PENGUIN  CLASSICS

BUDDHIST MEDITATION

KURTIS R. SCHAEFFER is a scholar and translator of Tibetan Buddhist literature. He is the Frances Myers Ball Professor of Religious Studies at the University of Virginia. He is the translator of and introducer for *The Life of the Buddha* by Tenzin Chögyel for Penguin Classics.

Buddhist Meditation

CLASSIC TEACHINGS FROM TIBET

Translated with an Introduction by
KURTIS R. SCHAEFFER

PENGUIN BOOKS

PENGUIN BOOKS

An imprint of Penguin Random House LLC
penguinrandomhouse.com

LIBRARY OF CONGRESS CATALOGING-IN-PUBLICATION DATA
Names: Schaeffer, Kurtis R., translator, compiler.
Title: Buddhist meditation : classic teachings from Tibet /
translated with an Introduction by Kurtis R. Schaeffer.
Description: 1st. | New York : Penguin Books, 2024. |
Includes bibliographical references.
Identifiers: LCCN 2023024940 (print) | LCCN 2023024941 (ebook) |
ISBN 9780143111467 (paperback) | ISBN 9781101992777 (ebook)
Subjects: LCSH: Meditation—Buddhism. | Buddhism—Tibet Region—Doctrines.
Classification: LCC BQ5625 .B83 2024 (print) | LCC BQ5625 (ebook) |
DDC 294.3/4432—dc23/eng/20231016
LC record available at https://lccn.loc.gov/2023024940
LC ebook record available at https://lccn.loc.gov/2023024941

Printed in the United States of America
1st Printing

Set in Sabon LT Pro

Contents

BUDDHIST MEDITATION

Introduction

AS YOU BEGIN

As you begin reading this book, pause to consider what makes up a given moment of thought. You can do this simply by looking at your own thoughts, right now, in this very moment. This is one of the hallmarks of human thought, the capacity for thought to turn around and look at itself working—the capacity to be self-aware. What range of ideas, objects, memories, plans are flowing through your consciousness at this moment? What range of emotions course through your mind and body as your thoughts turn from this idea to that memory, from this goal to that plan, from the sudden image of something you want, which is in turn replaced just as quickly by something you do not want, an image in your mind's eye of a thing, a task, a place, an experience that you want, or that you would just as soon avoid?

Take a moment to use the human capacity for self-consciousness to check in on your thoughts and emotions. What do you see? If you are like many people, you see—you feel—a great deal going on in your mind all at once. Yesterday's meeting at work, tomorrow's workout, that slightly antagonistic encounter with the mechanic over the cost of your car repair, next month's bills, or last year's vacation. These memories, plans, and images flash through your mind in rapid succession, overlapping at times, crowding each other out, competing for the attention of your front-most sense of consciousness, that specific "you" who experiences, who must deal with the assembly of thoughts that make up the larger, multitudinous "you."

And each of these thoughts may be yoked to a specific emotion—from expectant joy at the thought of meeting a friend to mild antipathy at the thought of meeting your competitor for the next promotion, from love at the arising of memories of friends and family during the holidays to gut-twisting dread at the thought of something truly catastrophic happening to one of them. At times this dense mixture of thought and emotion, as well as the physical impact this may have, is easy to handle. At other times it can be overwhelming.

Are there techniques for gaining a measure of control over our thoughts, emotions, and behaviors? Are there skills we can develop to enhance our mind's calm and focus? The contemplative traditions of Buddhism say yes.

MEDITATION

Buddhists have worked to be acutely aware of the machinations of our thoughts and emotions, and Buddhist traditions throughout the millennia and across Asia contain distinctive techniques and tools to bring them under greater control. We usually refer to these techniques with the English word *meditation*. And this is a good, powerful word that we will use throughout this book. Meditation in a general sense means cultivating control, flexibility, and focus in mind, emotion, and body. This training of the mind is, along with the pursuit to live an ethical life, the most important task that a Buddhist can undertake. The twentieth-century Tibetan Buddhist teacher Dudjom Rinpoche puts it simply: "Our benevolent teacher, the Buddha, says: 'Avoid every evil, practice perfect virtue, and fully train your mind: This is what the Buddha taught.' In line with this, if I were to summarize the goal of Buddhist training, it is that one must train one's own mind." Meditation and ethics—the training of the mind and the sustained effort to live virtuously for the benefit of ourselves and others—these are the intertwining ideals of Buddhist contemplative tradition.

Meditation comes in many forms, from simple to complex. Buddhists have been endlessly creative in developing powerful ways to train one's mind. Yet there are some important common starting points, and this is where this collection of meditation teachings is focused. A key technique to train in mental and emotional control, flexibility, and focus is to bring one's awareness to one's breath. The breath is an object of focus that we all have, so it serves as a free and easy point of reference for training in focus. If you have ever "taken a breath" to calm yourself, or to bring your mind back to the present moment or the task at hand, or to bring your emotions down from a heightened state, you have some experience with the usefulness of focusing on the breath. Bringing one's awareness back to one's breath whenever the mind wanders to some faraway memory, plan, or feeling is an essential common practice in Buddhism. We will read about this more in chapters 2 and 5.

Yet there is much more to meditation in Buddhism. Meditation can be about focus and calm, and it can also be about investigation and analysis. A standard way to describe this pair of techniques is "calm and insight" (in Sanskrit, *shamatha* and *vipashyana*). In calm meditation the practitioner uses techniques such as breath awareness to develop the capacity to calm one's mind and emotions—and, by extension, one's body. At first this sense of calm can be fleeting, shallow, and easily disturbed. Through practice, Buddhist meditation texts assure their readers, one can forge a deep calm that lasts for longer periods of time. Insight meditation makes use of an increased capacity for calm to focus the mind on features of mental, emotional, and embodied life. What is a thought? Where does a thought come from? How is it that it stays present, front and center in our consciousness? How and where does it recede? And what of emotions? How are they related to objects, images, memories? These are examples of the kinds of inquiry into one's mental and emotional experience that can be undertaken in insight meditation.

Buddhist meditation extends beyond calm and insight as well. Two Sanskrit terms that are often translated as "meditation" are *dhyana* and *bhavana*. Dhyana tends to range in meaning and practice from a withdrawal of the senses away from external objects and the movement toward states where thoughts about objects, be they physical or mental, are reduced to a minimum, to a kind of concentration where one utilizes the ability to withdraw from external objects of perception to focus on an idea or mental state. Dhyana tends to place emphasis on control of one's thoughts and awareness. Bhavana, by contrast, means cultivation, production, or development, and is more active in character. As "meditation," bhavana utilizes the power of calm to cultivate feelings of generosity toward others, or regret at one's past actions that may have led to the suffering of others. Bhavana can mean imagination, as in meditation practice that instructs the practitioner to generate a vivid image of a Buddha or Buddhist deity in front of oneself. This image should be so minutely and vividly constructed that it feels as if the divine figure were there, right in front of you. Bhavana meditation is active, constructive, creative.

Another important Sanskrit Buddhist term that is sometimes translated as "meditation" is *smriti*, or what is more commonly and better translated as "mindfulness." Mindfulness here can mean remembering a certain Buddhist teaching or ethical principle, or vigilance, for instance, of one's ethical commitments, or it can refer to the continuous practice of bringing one's awareness back to the object of focus. "Mindfulness of breath," then, means recalling one's awareness again and again back to a focus on the breath as the mind wanders. Other terms that are occasionally translated as "meditation" include the Sanskrit term *samadhi*, "concentration," and *pratipatti*, "practice," "accomplishment," or contemplation. Finally, common terms such as *to think* (Tibetan: *bsam*) can mean something closer to "meditation" in the context of teachings about Buddhist ethics and mental training.

The diversity of potential terms in Sanskrit that can usefully be translated by the English word *meditation* can give us some sense of the range of practices and skills that we might speak of when we speak about meditation. We can generally refer to meditation as mental training that combines calm and focus, though the range of techniques used to develop calm and focus, and the goals to which one can put an increased capacity for calm and focus, are wide indeed. Buddhism often uses the term *practice* or *contemplation* (Sanskrit: *pratipatti*, Tibetan: *sgrub pa*) to refer generally to the range of mental, emotional, and physical techniques that go into meditation. To this Buddhists contrast learning through scripture and texts (Sanskrit: *paryavapti*). Tibetan Buddhists use the term *khedrup*, "learned practitioner," to mean a person who is well read in books of philosophy and experienced in meditation. A khedrup is a "contemplative scholar," if you will.

This book uses *contemplation* to refer to this broader realm of Buddhist techniques for self-cultivation by working directly with the mind, the emotions, and the body. Tibetan Buddhism—like all traditions of Buddhism, from India to China, Japan, Korea, and Southeast Asia—has a rich contemplative culture, of which formal meditation is one part. This contemplative culture ranges from the large monastic universities with thousands of inhabitants to solitary meditators living, often for years at a time, alone in mountain retreat. Contemplative culture includes teachings on the nature of the mind, the nature of enlightenment—that unimaginably radical transformation of mind, body, self, and spirit that stands at the pinnacle of Buddhist views of person and cosmos—and it includes teachings on learning to control the everyday emotions that can get us in trouble, such as anger, pride, jealousy, and greed. And this contemplative culture threads together forms of knowledge and self-cultivation that are often treated separately in contemporary society. Where "learning" in the West is often deemed secular, and "meditation" spiritual or religious, in Tibet there is no such clear-cut distinction. Mental training and ethics, meditation and virtue are, ideally, both part and parcel of education.

Tibetan Buddhist tradition speaks of learning as a threefold process: learning, reflecting, and meditating. These are called the "three wisdoms." Learning is essential, from a Buddhist perspective, for developing an outlook on life that understands and takes seriously the challenge of simply being human. Without direct and deep engagement with the Buddhist classics of India, Tibetan writers argue, one misses out on the legacy of authoritative teachings on ethics, philosophy, and, yes, meditation. The first meditations presented in this book, in chapters 2, 3, and 4, for instance, touch on some of the topics that are fundamental to Buddhist learning: the inescapable reality of human suffering, the ways in which we create our own experience of reality through repeated patterns of behavior (i.e., karma), the possibility of changing these negative patterns, and, ultimately, the possibility—however distant—of completely overcoming human suffering (nirvana, or enlightenment). Yet it is not enough to simply learn by rote Buddhist philosophy or ethics; the student of Buddhism must reflect on the ways in which Buddhist viewpoints on human life play out in one's own life. This critical analysis puts philosophy to the test, challenging it to tell us something worthwhile about how we live, how we go astray, and how we correct ourselves to develop more fully as humans who recognize the basic goodness that we are capable of and, more crucially, the fundamental importance of others. And how are learning and critical reflection actuated? How are they integrated into the fabric of our lives, our view of ourselves, and our behavior toward others? Through meditation. Without meditation, learning and critical reflection are inert; they are incapable of effecting any real change in our lives. In this context, meditation is the process of applying thought to the problem of being human through the careful cultivation of our innate yet undeveloped powers of mind, emotion, and body.

THE TEACHINGS

Buddhist Meditation: Classic Teachings from Tibet offers accessible and authentic selections from the most important and influential meditation instructions of Tibetan Buddhism. The anthology includes classic contemplative exercises on the opportunities and challenges of life; cultivating inner calm; fostering a wider perspective on oneself in relationship to others; and working with negative emotions and the highest values of the Buddhist tradition, love and compassion. Several dozen meditation instructions are collected in twelve chapters, each highlighting a distinct theme within Tibet's rich contemplative literature. *Buddhist Meditation* presents an engaging introduction to traditional teachings on meditation. All major traditions of Tibetan Buddhism are represented in this brief book. Each work is freshly translated for this volume, and most appear here in English for the first time.

Collectively, *Buddhist Meditation* offers a general introduction to classic teachings from the contemplative culture of Tibet. The structure of the book loosely follows what in Tibet are known as "foundation practices," practice manuals that immerse the reader in the search for meaningful and compassionate responses to the ubiquity of human suffering, and in the contemplative techniques that translate that search into consequential action. The first part of these foundation practice manuals introduce students to four topics of contemplation: (1) the unique and fundamentally valuable opportunity that human existence provides each and every person for self-betterment and—always aligned with self-development— the opportunity to be of benefit to other living beings; (2) the inescapable persistence of suffering in life, and the reality of death; (3) the workings of ethical cause and effect, otherwise known as karma, upon our behaviors and experiences of life; and (4) the ever-repeating succession of frustration known as cyclic existence, or samsara. Together, these spiritual exercises are intended to cultivate a sense of detachment from the world, quickened by a sense that continuing to desire the goals of the world will result in more dissatisfaction than satisfaction, more suffering than solace, more sorrow than joy.

The second set of foundation practices is quite different in character. It provides tools to build on the foundation of heightened existential sensitivity to life's transience formed in the first set. These tools include (5) taking refuge in Buddhism—a deep formal commitment to integrate Buddhist contemplative and ethical teachings into one's life; (6) cultivating love and compassion for all living beings; (7) clearing away cognitive, emotional, and behavioral impediments to actualizing love and compassion; (8) developing with wisdom and the experience and excellent qualities necessary to put love and compassion into practice; and (9) dedicating oneself to a spiritual mentor to serve as a guide through this intensive program of training. Where the first group of foundation practices offers techniques with which to transform one's intellectual orientation to living, the second set introduces physical and imaginative techniques to intended to deepen that orientation through embodied practice.

Part existential philosophy, part ethics, part self-help program, part cosmology—the foundation exercises present a complete Buddhist picture of life, the ethical universe, and the first steps in making a positive impact in life for ourselves and others, steps anyone can begin to take by dedicating themselves to train in contemplative exercises. These exercises constitute a well-rounded Buddhist practice in and of themselves, and Buddhist teachers typically say that one is never finished building the "foundation" for an ethically motivated life; it is a lifelong pursuit, so one never stops working through the foundation practices. But the foundation practices are foundational, or perhaps "preliminary," as their name in Tibetan is sometimes translated, in one important respect; the existential and ethical formation that these practices are designed to develop are fundamental to other types of meditation practice, including the meditations presented in chapters 5, 6, and 9.

This book draws liberally from the Tibetan Buddhist foundation practices. Chapters 3, 5, 6, and 8 are each drawn from foundation practice manuals. The other chapters treat related topics, sometimes extending the conversation in different directions, sometimes offering a fresh perspective on the same material through such techniques as poetry or dialogue exercises. Collectively, the selections from works translated in these chapters cover six of the nine foundation practices listed above: (1) the opportunity of being human; (2) suffering in life and death; (3) ethical cause and effect; (4) the frustrations of cyclic existence; (5) taking refuge in Buddhism; and (6) cultivating love and compassion for all living beings.

Foundation practice manuals exist in every school of Tibetan Buddhism, and each offers a distinctive arrangement and expression of the individual contemplative practices as well as a view of the nature of the mind that is unique to that school. In traditional settings the student dedicated to sustained meditation practice would follow the foundation practices of their own school under the close guidance of their spiritual adviser, who should possess deep experience in those practices. As part of a secular series of books (the Penguin Classics series), this book can offer selections from different schools as it presents meditations and contemplative literature drawn from the foundation practices and elsewhere. Authors from all the major schools of Tibetan Buddhism, including the Geluk, Kagyu, and Nyingma, Sakya and the Jonang schools, all appear here. Each of these schools has a deep contemplative literature of its own; what is presented here is merely a sampling of one thousand years of a richer and more diverse literature on meditation than any single volume can represent. Historically, the works range from the early poetry of Milarepa, who was active in the twelfth century, to the near-contemporary foundation practice manual of the twentieth-century teacher from the Jonang School, Ngawang Yönten Gyatso. In between, major writers and teachers from the fourteenth through nineteenth centuries all find a place here.

If there is a featured writer here, it is poet and lifelong mountain contemplative Shabkar Tsokdruk Rangdröl. None of the pieces excerpted here from his massive collection of writings come from a foundation practice manual, but they have everything to do with meditation and the contemplative culture in which meditators thrive. Shabkar's poetry begins the volume and forms the centerpiece of the final trio of chapters dedicated to the joys of the contemplative life—a wide-ranging and heartfelt ode to the trials and triumphs of meditation in mountain retreat.

THE CHAPTERS

Chapter 1, "To the Mountain," centers us in the mountains of Tibet. The mountain retreat is a real place—thousands of real places, in fact—dotting the highways and byways of valleys and peaks throughout the Himalayas, the high plains of central Tibet, and the high mountain pasturelands and forested ravines of eastern Tibet. The mountain retreat is also an imagined place, the ideal realm for meditation, far from the madding crowd of family, town, and village life, and removed as well from the dry intellectualism of the great Buddhist monastic universities of Tibet. The mountain retreat symbolizes the highest aspirations of Tibetan Buddhist contemplative culture as well as the most serious challenges that the work of meditation can place upon an individual: the challenge of confronting oneself as an individual, solitary, alone, unprotected from the buzz and cover usually provided by the frenetic action and cacophony of daily life "down the mountain," in society, among other human beings. The poems here orient us to the contemplative culture of Buddhism in Tibet.

In chapter 2, "At the Foot of the Tree," the Thirteenth Dalai Lama offers introductory orientation to the techniques of seating and posture for meditation. This teaching is part of a longer address to monks gathered for the New Year's celebrations in Lhasa, the capital city of Tibet, in the early twentieth century. The Dalai Lama gave such teachings annually to novice and master monks alike. They are a kind of "introduction to Buddhism" for monks, providing a basic how-to for beginning meditation, as well as a primer on the life of the Buddha that focuses on his final place of meditation before his enlightenment. The Dalai Lama offers a basic orientation to Buddhist values and outlook on life, which serves here as a preface for the topics presented in chapter 3.

In chapter 3, "Living and Dying," the eighteenth-century text *The Source of All Attainment* by Yeshé Gyeltsen, tutor to the Eighth Dalai Lama, takes the reader through a meditation on mortality, as well as reasons to be joyful for the great opportunity that human life affords for growth in expanding areas of activity: one's own healthy sense of self, one's relationships with others, and within the larger goal of reframing one's existence so that it prioritizes the well-being and happiness of others. More specifically, Yeshé Gyeltsen introduces us to the first of the foundation practices. As with so many of the works translated here, each theme, each passage is worthy of lingering on, for while the topics do build upon each other, each also suggests a unique way of investigating our own experiences, our own behaviors. Reading slowly, taking time to consider how we might work the guided contemplations that Yeshé Gyeltsen offers into our own reflections, perhaps makes best use of writing such as this.

In chapter 4, "Songs of Impermanence," Shabkar picks up the theme of impermanence, which Yeshé Gyeltsen presented in comparatively reserved prose, and explores the experience of transience through poetic brevity, imagery, and metaphor.

With a sense of both the possibility and the urgency of self-development fully integrated into one's way of approaching the world, Buddhist contemplative systems turn to more structured methods of meditations. Chapter 5, "Inner Calm," and chapter 6, "Wider Perspective," offer detailed instructions in the two primary types of formal meditation presented in this volume, calm and insight meditations. The great sixteenth-century philosopher and scholar from the Sakya School, Ngorchen Könchok Lhündrup, presents a clear and concise instruction on calm meditation in his famous work, *The Ornament of the Three Visions*. In *Dispelling the Darkness of Ignorance*, the equally famous Ninth Karmapa Wangchuk Dorjé introduces insight meditation, and details multiple contemplative exercises designed to lead the practitioner through an investigation of one's own patterns of thought and emotion. Where the Sakya scholar tends to see meditation as the development of new skills, new ways of being grounded in oneself and less bound to the lure of images, ideas, and other objects of desire, the Kagyu scholar portrays meditation to be a process of uncovering the human mind's natural capacity to be vividly aware of being alive in the present moment. The two chapters, each from a different school of Tibetan Buddhist thought, thus give us two views of the spiritual progress—one that argues that we must walk intentionally along a path to move our thoughts, our behaviors, and our emotions from a state of suffering to a state of joy, and one that argues that we have never left this state of joy but do not recognize this. This tension runs throughout Buddhist contemplative thought in Tibet and elsewhere. And while the premises and techniques may be distinctive, the goal is the same in these two contemplative systems—to overcome suffering for oneself and others.

Chapter 7, "Ourselves and Others," is a version of one of the most gripping contemplative exercises in all of Buddhism—a dialogue between you and . . . you. This scripted meditation asks the practitioner to take on the role of another person and then to look back at oneself through the eyes of that person. What do you see? How do you feel about "yourself," seeing for the first time your behaviors, your expressions, your world from the perspective of another? And all the while knowing what "you" think about "you," for the role-playing and dialogue all occur within the vast and varied space of your own thoughts. Ethics is a key topic of meditation of Buddhism, though unlike more didactic philosophical writings, contemplative dialogues offer tools to cultivate, and perhaps more important, to *experiment* with ethically charged modes of relating to others. This excerpt from Shenpen Tayé's *Notes on Shantideva's Way of the Bodhisattva* includes several meditations on ourselves in relation to others, including the famous practice of imaginatively putting oneself in the place of another so that, while your happiness becomes theirs, you heroically take on their suffering. Here the mind directly confronts its propensity for selfishness, asking itself, "Can you afford to be selfish?"

Chapter 8, "Cosmic Love," returns to the foundation practices, this time focusing on love, compassion, empathetic joy,
and equanimity (part of foundation practice six). These contemplations present classic Buddhist teachings on the central-
ity of love, both for our relationships with others and for our
own spiritual growth. From a Buddhist perspective, the answer, plain and simple, to the question, "How should I re-
spond to the suffering caused by people's negative behaviors?"
(a question posed in foundation practices two through four)
is love and compassion. If the preliminary contemplations at
the end of chapter 1 and throughout chapters 3 and 4 illustrate that suffering is endemic to human existence, then chapter 7's exchange of self and other illustrates that every human
being feels the weight of this burden. In these meditations on
cosmic love, the practitioner makes the decision to think and
act with sympathy rather than antipathy toward others, precisely because they, like us, experience suffering yet yearn for
happiness. The ideal Buddhist response to this is to vow to
become a "bodhisattva," a being dedicated to becoming enlightened precisely to alleviate the sufferings of others. Chapter 8 presents a basic set of contemplative techniques for
training as a bodhisattva.

Chapter 9, "Open Mind, Vast Mind," returns to themes
first explored in chapters 5 and 6, calm meditation and insight meditation. These lively and humane meditations on
the inherently positive potential of the human mind were
written by one of Tibet's most famous meditation teachers,
the nineteenth-century master from eastern Tibet, Patrul
Rinpoche. Patrul's *Naturally Liberated Meditation* contains
a dozen pieces of advice on the contemplative life, offered in
a blend of disarmingly direct poetry and prose. Like the
Kagyu teacher, the Ninth Karmapa, of chapter 6's teaching
on insight meditation, Patrul portrays meditation as the uncovering and releasing of our mind's natural vibrance, vital-
ity, and clarity. Sounding much like a Zen teacher from
China, Japan, or Korea, Patrul's refrain throughout these
teachings is that, in reality, there is nothing "to be done" in

meditation. There is no new state of mind that we do not already have and are able to experience as a lived reality—if only we can pause deeply enough to notice it, to let it emerge from the morass of our otherwise frenetic thought, emotions, and behaviors. "Just let it be," counsels Patrul; let the mind be itself, without trying to push it in one direction or another, or to make it something that it is not. These informal pieces of advice and philosophical reflection can be profitably read in conjunction with the more formal instructions of chapters 5 and 6.

The final three chapters return to where the volume began, to the solitude of the contemplative mountain retreat. This time, however, we bring the ethical frame and meditation instructions of Buddhist contemplative culture up the mountain with us as we explore different facets of mountain retreat in more detail. The works on meditation presented in this book are "Tibetan" in great part because of this environmental frame, as opposed to Indian, Chinese, Japanese, Thai, or Sri Lankan—one of the many regions of the Buddhist world in which distinctive contemplative traditions have developed and flourished. The mountains are an ever-present feature of Tibet, and Tibetan writers were keenly aware of their symbolic power. To go to meditate was, since the time of Milarepa in the twelfth century, to go "up the mountain," to take advantage of everything that the high peaks and pure earth of Tibet's transcendent landscape afford to those seeking the "solitude," however real or symbolic, that Buddhism assures will aid meditation.

The mountains of Tibet are an iconic image in the Tibetan vision of Buddhist contemplative culture. They represent the sublime possibility that humans can transcend their ingrained patterns of thought and behavior, that they can rise above the petty yet destructive entanglements that people seem bound to engage in "down" in the village, the town, or the city. The mountains represent the utopian vision that a person can rise above their current image of themselves as inherently separate from all other people to reach new vistas upon the collective life of humanity. The final three chapters dig deep into the specifics of mountain retreats by looking at the places one should meditate, the challenges to successful meditation, and the joys of meditation and a contemplative life.

The selections in these final three chapters are intended to convey something of this wide-open vision of human life. Chapter 10, "Places of Solitude," asks, Where should one meditate? While any location should, in principle, be suitable for contemplative practice, Tibetan tradition praises the natural seclusion to be found in the mountains and high valleys of the Himalayas. Fourteenth-century author Longchen Rabjam details what to look for when assessing a good location for retreat in this passage from his manual of Buddhist contemplation, *Chariot of Knowledge: A Commentary on the Comfort and Ease of Meditation*.

Chapter 11, "The Trials of Solitude," presents a complete translation of Shabkar's responses to questions from a disciple in contemplative retreat. Through the honest questions of Shabkar's disciple, we hear the apprehension that any would-be practitioner might feel when beginning a program of meditation. What if I get sick while I am meditating? What if there is no one around to teach me? What if I am scared? How do I engage with friends, family, the social world if I am ensconced in a contemplative practice? Will this make any positive difference in the world? To each of these concerns Shabkar answers with a supportive, positive affirmation that his disciple can succeed in the contemplative life. And while Shabkar's advice is geared, at least on the surface, toward someone heading into the mountains, the apprehensions and questions addressed here are applicable to many times and places in which one finds oneself on the brink of contemplative practice. Shabkar's work, more than most in the tradition, takes the sheer challenge of meditation seriously, pointing out specific trials that the meditator may face when journeying "to the mountain." It is also among the most joyously positive works on preparing for meditation—You can do it! says Shabkar.

Finally, chapter 12, "Sheer Joy," brings the volume to a close with songs from a unique version of the life and songs of Milarepa known as *The Black Treasury*. These songs express the sheer joy encountered after one has made that leap from beginning a contemplative practice to dwelling within it. Milarepa's songs echo from the meditation retreats of centuries of Tibetan contemplative masters. There just is nothing else like it, proclaims Milarepa—the simple opportunity to sequester oneself, even for a moment, so that one may move from the work of the world to work on oneself. This is the joy of working on one's mind. One's emotional life. One's way of being with others. One's whole being. What the Buddha began on the plains of India millennia ago, Milarepa continues on the high slopes of the Himalayas. Here he offers encouragement to anyone with songs of joy that say, Come along! To the mountain. To the foot of the tree. To the meditation seat.

TRANSLATION

Each work here is translated from the original Tibetan source. Some works integrate verse and prose from Indian Buddhist works composed in Sanskrit, though the translations of these, too, are from the Tibetan sources in which such passages appear. There are no notes accompanying these translations. Each one deserves extended annotation, especially because Tibetan-language meditation terminology is often only shallowly understood outside of contexts where experienced Tibetan teachers have elaborated on the often subtle details of this unique lexicon, and because the English language that attempts to capture the richness of meaning in the Tibetan has had only a few decades to develop, as opposed to the centuries in which Tibetans crafted this vocabulary. Every translation is an experiment in understanding and communication that attempts to capture something of lived experience in a useful manner, and it is in this spirit that the translations here are offered. Notes on the details may be found in books listed in Sources and Suggestions for Further Reading.

The translations make liberal use of section headings to aid the reader. While some works, such as the Ninth Karmapa's *Dispelling the Darkness of Ignorance* in chapter 6, do have outlines of their own that translate into useful section headings, others do not, such as the Thirteenth Dalai Lama's teachings in chapter 2, which is very close to an oral teaching that flows easily from topic to topic. Some texts, such as Yeshé Gyeltsen's work on living and dying in chapter 3, have some section headings, but these give little indication of the distinct contemplative exercises that this text presents. Individual exercises are marked out with asterisks (***), indicating a good place to pause and reflect on the significance of the given exercise and its theme.

Most Tibetan Buddhist songs of spiritual experience do not have titles, so poem names have been added for clarity, and to suggest to the reader possible themes to focus on within the poem.

Introductions to each chapter orient readers to the distinctive subject matter and context of the translated work. Introductions also offer orientation on the practical application and significance of the chapter for readers, relating the content of the classic works to contemporary human challenges and possibilities. The Sources and Suggestions for Further Reading sections provide complete references for all Tibetan-language texts translated here, as well as for previous translations. It also offers suggestions for next readings to complement the works in each of the twelve chapters.

This collection includes a good deal of verse, and quite a bit of that is poetry. Verse, in the Buddhist tradition, is regularly metered speech; it uses metered rhythmical lines. Buddhists have composed in verse almost since the early days of the tradition. It is useful for its brevity and concision, being more economical than prose. Metered speech is also relatively easy to memorize, meaning that you can "take it with you" into a quick meditation session, or a longer contemplative retreat. Poetry is metered verse that is also intentionally eloquent, using the full range of rhythmic, aural, and semantic devices available in the language. Buddhists have also written poetry over and above verse, since the initial moments of the tradition in Indian, and in every country in which Buddhism has flourished. End rhyming is not typical in this tradition of poetry, though alliteration and assonance are common. These aural techniques help to breathe life into the Tibetan original, though the translations here make no attempt to capture this, concentrating instead on the imagery used in the poems.

Tibetan writers were keen students of Indian poetry, studying Sanskrit verse and eloquent speech both for their aesthetic joys and as models for developing a poetic tradition in Tibet. Beginning with Milarepa in the twelfth century, Tibetan contemplatives took up poetry as a primary vehicle to convey the experience of meditation. They heralded the joy they felt from meditation, or the vibrant sense of luminous awareness felt when scattered thoughts cease darting around the mind and one's consciousness settles into tranquility. They praised the places of meditation and the precious moments that they eked out from their social lives to sit down and practice. They also used poetry as a contemplative technology, a set of tools and techniques not only for describing meditation, but for doing meditation. Poetry in Tibetan Buddhist contemplative culture is meditative. The rhythm of poetry slows the mind down, focusing it on the flow of language, the sheer aural, palpitating sensuality of the words catching the attention of our thoughts long enough to reflect on how their meanings might relate to our lives. And the language of poetry, in turn, is language specifically intended to enhance our capacity for imaginative and metaphorical thought. Mind doesn't exactly "shimmer" in the sense that sunlight on the lake surface might, though metaphors of light and its evanescent movement are long-standing language-based techniques for attempting to capture a vibrancy of human awareness that so many contemplatives have declared to be found deep in the heart of meditation. Throughout these translations, poetry is treated not just as a vehicle for instruction about meditation, but as a kind of meditation in and of itself.

And yet aside from language, poetic or otherwise, there is something about meditation that works to escape being pinned down in words. The experience of meditation is often said in Tibetan Buddhist tradition to be ineffable, to be beyond the capacity of language to capture experience. Sometimes it is said that language can only point in the general direction of contemplative experience. Others say that language points in precisely the wrong direction, that the very act of defining or describing already means that one has gone down the wrong path. The larger issue, perhaps, about reading or talking about meditation is not that it misses the mark, but that meditation is a form of human activity that is distinct from reading and talking. There are times, contemplative times if you will, where language appears to fall away from the experience of being, right here, right now, with oneself. Of being, simply, oneself. "Let it be," as Patrul says. Perhaps this is a cautionary teaching about the limits of language itself. It is thus that an anthology of writings about meditation cannot be assembled without a certain sense of irony— but of course, no more irony than one might ascribe to the fact that, for over a thousand years, Tibetan Buddhists have penned untold numbers of texts on an activity that is at once so tantalizingly elusive and so concretely present, the first-person exploration of human consciousness in meditation.

KURTIS R. SCHAEFFER

Buddhist Meditation

CHAPTER ONE

TO THE MOUNTAIN

INTRODUCTION

The most elegant literature about meditation is surely the song of spiritual experience. Ever since the great poet-saint Milarepa sang his songs of meditation and realization in the twelfth century, Tibetan meditators have spoken of their contemplative experience in song. Many of these were indeed meant to be sung. They were sung to students entering practices of meditation. They were sung by large groups as a sort of collective praise of the contemplative life and those who lived it. And they were sung by meditators to themselves as encouragement.

Spiritual songs were also poetry, composed to be read, reread, savored, and scrutinized. The tradition of Buddhist spiritual poetry is over a thousand years old in Tibet, though its sources stretch back both to the Buddhist poets of India and to ancient folk poetry of Tibet. From Indian Buddhism Tibetan writers gained an acute sense of rendering experiences of the mind in meditation through a combination of meditation terms and poetic devices. Here, philosophical ideas about the nature of the mind are fused with rich imagery drawn from the natural world. From Tibetan folk song, it gained a visceral use of rhythm and a playful sense of humor, and a vibrant set of imagery drawn from the snowcapped Himalayas, the high mountain grassy plains, and the deep blue lakes that adorn the Tibetan plateau. Some of the most famous works of all Tibetan literature, and some of the most famous meditation teachings of Tibetan Buddhism, are in the form of spiritual song.

After Milarepa (whom we shall hear from elsewhere in this book), the most famous poet-saint is Shabkar (Shabkar Tsokdruk Rangdröl, 1781–1851). Born in the northeastern Tibetan region of Amdo, Shabkar traveled the length and breadth of Tibet to undertake extensive meditation retreats in the famous hermitages of the Himalayas. He dedicated collections of spiritual song to every place he stayed through-out his long life. When these were finally collected by his disciples at the end of his life, they amounted to the largest collection of contemplative poetry ever known to Tibet. In this chapter as well as chapters 4 and 11, we will hear just a few choice examples of Shabkar's verse from his collection of over a thousand poems.

Shabkar used spiritual song to teach about many aspects of Buddhism, and to many different audiences. He spoke of meditation, of course, yet he also spoke of ethical living, the challenges of our social worlds, the nature of the mind and cosmos, and the importance of living a full human life. His collection of Buddhist poems became hugely popular, able to be taken up and enjoyed by everyone, from experienced full-time meditators in retreat to novices balancing the needs of daily life with the desire to undertake spiritual work. His work was read throughout the Himalayas, and today it is not unusual to see everyone from a nun in meditation retreat to a shop clerk minding the store reading Shabkar's and Milarepa's songs.

Among Shabkar's very favorite topics is the mountain retreat. He simply loved to describe, in soaring verse, the beauties of hermitages, bastions of the contemplative life, as well as mountains, valleys, and landscapes that formed the ideal contexts for meditation. In Shabkar's poetry the mountain retreat becomes a feast for the senses, the mind, and emotions. The water is pure; the fields and forests pungent with aromatic herbs; the lakeshores dotted with deer, gazelles, and yaks; and the air alive with the buzzing of bees and the sweet song of birds.

These places are the ideal settings for successful meditation. Natural beauty, quiet, distance from the complexities of social life—the mountain retreat offers many advantages to the hermit. In the first poem on the next page, Shabkar lists the benefits of mountain retreats: no thieves, full of herb gardens, birds and animals, pure water, caves, wild fruits and vegetables, and the enduring memory of the honored hermits who have sat in these places throughout the generations.

The second poem offers a humorous look at the different kinds of meditators one might encounter in retreat. Or perhaps these are tendencies of thought and behavior one might see in oneself? "Wandering Fox Meditator" fixates on food, wondering too much about the next meal. "Roaming Dog Meditator" worries too much about money, always searching for the next coin, the next dollar. Can we recognize such patterns of thought in ourselves? Shabkar offers playful imagery to do just that.

The final poem in this chapter brings the power of metaphor to the work of imagining what it is to be in mountain retreat, to live the contemplative life. The sky is "wide open," spacious, without boundary or center. Too many words, Shabkar cautions, places limits on contemplation, tries to give shape and limit to the sky where there are none. Can we take up this metaphor as a powerful technique to imagine what openness in meditation might mean, might be like?

Occasionally Shabkar mentions specific traditions of contemplative thought and practice, such as the Great Seal, Great Perfection, Central Way, and so forth. Do not worry about these too much. Some will come up in later chapters, and all can be found in the readings listed at the end of the book. Rather, focus on his use of poetic language to evoke the depth and richness of the Tibetan meditation traditions. As you read Shabkar's poems in this opening chapter, let the metaphor, simile, and imagery sit with you. Shabkar's songs are all about meditation—the places that make ideal settings for meditation, or the thoughts and behaviors that one can encounter in meditation. Yet they are not instructional works in the way that later chapters are; there is no instruction on proper posture here (we will hear about this in chapter 2), or on the ethics of giving (which we will also encounter in chapter 7). These playful songs instead provide us with tools for creative thought, for imagining what meditation is and how we might start to approach it. Only after we have sat with Shabkar for a moment "in mountain retreat," briefly considering the power of imagination and creative play, will we begin exploring the working details of meditation in the following chapter.

In Mountain Retreat

To the ancestors, who turned their backs on the delusions
    of this life,
Who made meditation traditions—
Great Seal, Great Perfection, Central Way, Pacification,
    Severance—
Central to their experience
And achieved spiritual realization, I bow.

Listen as I speak of the good qualities of mountain
    retreat,
Those places rippling with the power of the holy ones
    of old,
Close to Heaven, where you are happy, where you
    experience joy.
I go to meditate in mountain retreat.

At the top of the mountain the land is pure.
No thieves will harm you.
You'll have unspoiled contentment, and
Joyous contemplation.
A long life without illness.
Its good qualities are incredible!
I go to meditate in mountain retreat.

Amid snowy peaks,
Are herb gardens and forested lands,
Full of beautiful birds and animals.
Pure water streams down, bubbling
    forth.
I go to meditate in mountain retreat.

Broad-leaved trees decked with fruit and
    flowers,
Rustle when the fair wind catches them.
Bees make the wildflowers sing and dance.
I go to meditate in mountain retreat.

The mountain has rocky caves, fruit trees,
A cool summer hut,
Wild sweet potato, green vegetables,
Sweet and tasty summer food.
I've gone to meditate in mountain retreat.

A place brimming with the power of the holy ones
    of old,
A place where the devout live this very moment,
A place where the Buddha's children will emerge
    someday.
I've gone to meditate in mountain retreat.

A place where masters, meditation gods, and celestial
    muses meet,
Where dharma defenders, guardian spirits, and local
    gods roam,
A place of both common and extraordinary merits.
I've gone to meditate in mountain retreat.

So here is a song that speaks a bit
Of the good qualities of the hermitage.
I sang this when I went to the mountain.
Through what virtue it has, may I and everyone else,

Go up to the mountain and gain spiritual insight.

I sang this song just to make myself happy.

❀ ❀ ❀ ❀ ❀

Wandering Fox, Roaming Dog

Buddha turned the dharma wheel
Long ago.
Today in these fallen times,
I, but a beggar, bow in faith
To the Buddha and the masters,
Who granted the dharma to me.

If I don't teach with a few illustrations,
It may be difficult for some of you to grasp.
So I'll use images to make the point.
Listen now to my harmonious song.

Fox wanders the desolate valley,
Hoping to find food.
Have you wondered,
"Where is my next meal?"
As you've wandered up to the mountain retreat?
If so, you are
Wandering Fox Meditator!

Dog circles the temple,
Wondering,
"Can I grab some food?"
Have you wondered,
"Where is my next coin?"
While roaming far-off lands?
If so, you are
Roaming Dog Meditator!

Old Owl sits on the rock and hoots.
Do you sit upon your rock,
Spouting twisted dharma stories to others?
If so, you are
Old Owl Meditator!

Wild Grouse sits up on the hill.
Do you sit high up in your retreat,
Taking profound dharma into your experience?
If so, you are
Wild Grouse Meditator!

Snow Lion lives up on the glacier,
Pouncing, jumping, leaping in air.
Do you perfect your spiritual strength in mountain
     retreat,
Attaining the heights of the three spiritual bodies?
If so, you are
White Lion Meditator!

Vulture sits on the cliff, then soars into space.
Do you meditate single-pointedly on the cliff,
Traveling ever higher to Buddha realms?
If so, you are
Vulture Meditator!

Sun above dispels the darkness in every land.
Do you wander the kingdoms,
Bringing benefit to people and the dharma alike?
If so, you are
Sun Above Meditator!

Jewel brings all you need if you dig it up.
Do you make offerings and prayers,
Bestowing a treasury of accomplishments,
Both simple and sublime?
If so, you are
Jewel Meditator!

By whatever merit there is in singing this song,
May Lion, Bird, Grouse, Sun, and Jewel—
May every kind of meditator,
Carefree and mutually committed to dharma,
Come to fill this entire high mountain retreat.

I sang this to some disciples who had entered mountain
    retreat to meditate, including the faithful treasurer of
    Purang, the caretaker Achok Ladakh Khenpo, and the
    monk Orgyen.

❀ ❀ ❀ ❀ ❀

Become Mountain

Sky
Carefree Shabkar,
You revel in words.
But try taking a cue from the
Wide-open sky.
Give yourself over to a meditation
Without boundaries, without center.

When the dark southern clouds gather,
No special effort is needed to clear them away.
Southern clouds are just visions in the sky.

Become Sky.
Be its nature.
Liberation will come naturally,
Have no doubt.

Mountain
You, free and easy bard,
Take a cue from

The mountain at Lakeheart.
Give yourself over to an unshakable meditation.

When the berry bushes bloom,
They need no extra force to fade away.
The forest is just a vision on the mountain.

Become Mountain.
Be its nature.
Liberation will come naturally,
Have no doubt.

Lake
You, Mountain Man, wandering and wild,
Take a cue from
Lake Trishok.
Give yourself to meditation that is
Stillness all the way down.

When many waves are crashing,
They need no outside influence to settle down,
Waves are just a vision upon the lake.

Become Lake Trishok.
Be its nature.
Liberation will come naturally,
Have no doubt.

Awareness
You, a yogin of the Great Perfection,
Give yourself to meditation without concepts,
As you nurture this intrinsic awareness,
Infinite and unimpeded.

When your thoughts get out of hand,
Be they good or bad,
They need no analysis to settle down.
Thoughts are just a vision of intrinsic awareness.

Become Awareness.
Be its nature.
Liberation will come naturally,
Have no doubt.

I, the aimless wanderer Tsokdruk Rangdröl, sang this
song to myself at Lakeheart.

CHAPTER TWO

AT THE FOOT OF THE TREE

INTRODUCTION

Meditation begins with body and breath. The body should in most cases be both relaxed and ready—relaxed so that one can bring one's mind to whatever focus of attention one wants, and ready to adjust to changes in thought, emotion, and physical feeling that affect meditation. Buddhists have developed easy-to-follow instructions for taking up and adjusting bodily posture, and for integrating breathing into contemplation. Yet if they are easy to follow, they are not simplistic, for teachings on body and breath form the basis for all subsequent meditation teachings. More than that, basic posture and breathing techniques are practices that can grow in depth over time. They are practices in their own right, with their own unique complexity, even as they are requisites for more cognitively involved contemplations.

The text translated in this chapter introduces the basics of Buddhist meditation posture and simple breath awareness practice, as well as motivation for beginning a meditation practice. Along the way it hints at the wider world of Buddhist thought and practice in which sitting and breath meditations are located. The author of this brief introduction to meditation is none other than one of the famous Dalai Lamas.

The Thirteenth Dalai Lama, Tubten Gyatso (1876–1933) was, in addition to being a tireless statesman amid a tumultuous time in East Asian history, a consummate preacher.

For decades he taught at the annual New Year's festivities in Lhasa, speaking on topics ranging from introductory meditation instructions to ritual life to ethics to more involved practices of contemplative visualization. In 1924 he offered an introduction to the basics of meditation, beginning with posture. His teachings to the many monks who had come to Lhasa to celebrate the New Year provide a clear explanation of the traditional cross-legged meditation posture, as well as a few variants for those who find that other ways of sitting are more agreeable to their situation.

The Thirteenth Dalai Lama contextualizes meditation, and the focus on ideal seating and posture, within the long history of Buddhism, stretching back to the contemplative techniques of the Buddha himself. He tells the story of the Buddha's search for the right place and the right seating material, where he would achieve the singular experience that the Buddhist dharma is founded upon, the enlightenment—a radical transformation of mind, body, and emotion in which the relationships among self, others, and cosmos are redefined so fundamentally that suffering ceases to exist.

This utopian vision of human possibility begins with a humble grass seat under a tree. The Buddha took advantage of the comforting softness of a grass seat, and the cooling shade of the broad-leaved pipal tree. But the details of the Buddha's story are just that—details in an ancient narrative that may have been applicable then in ways they are not today. The kusha grass that the Buddha sat on is, most likely, difficult to come by today. (And the Dalai Lama's audience had likely never set eyes on kusha grass, for that matter!) The larger point of the Dalai Lama's teaching is that attention to the details of how we comport ourselves during meditation matters. We pay attention to our bodies during meditation; the details about posture help us to do so in a focused, consistent manner. We use the rhythms of our body to bring the mind back to the present; the breath is our ultimate source of rhythm, always available to us, always there for us to gently return our minds to.

The concluding section of the Dalai Lama's sermon offers a preview of issues to come in the following chapters, including motivations for meditation, the nature of human pleasure and pain, and the importance of mind and emotions for nearly every aspect of personal and collective life. The Dalai Lama emphasizes what Buddhism takes to be the central existential challenge: human mortality. He does so by introducing a key Buddhist idea, cyclic existence (or *samsara* in Sanskrit). Cyclic existence is the life each of us lives for ourselves, and the life each of us shares together. We are born, we live, we die—and if you are Buddhist, you hold that you are reborn only to live, age, die, and be reborn again and again, without end. The problem with this is that cyclic existence is characterized, on balance, by experiences of pervasive dissatisfaction and of acute physical and emotional suffering. In the Buddhist view of human life, there is no greater tragedy than the fact that we perpetually exist in this state of suffering. And to compound matters, Buddhism argues that it is our own thoughts and emotions that cause us suffering, no more and no less. This is the motivation for meditation; by meditating, Buddhism holds, we can train our minds and emotions to produce less suffering for ourselves and others. (Buddhism does allow for misfortune and chance, so suffering is not actually all one's fault, but this nuance is not typically included in discussions of motivation.) The Dalai Lama introduces this topic to us and provides us the basic tools to begin to address the topic: posture and breathing. The following chapters will pick up where the Dalai Lama leaves off, moving us from the body and breath to mind, emotions, and the challenges of human experience.

The Dalai Lama includes a section on esoteric, or tantric, Buddhist practice, in which the practitioner creatively works with energies in the body to enhance contemplative progress. Breathing and posture skills are a prerequisite for this range of practices, and while this anthology does not include any such meditations, the Dalai Lama does provide a good sense here of the kinds of advanced meditations that practitioners might train for using the foundation practices described throughout the chapters.

TEACHINGS FOR THE NEW YEAR, BY THE THIRTEENTH DALAI LAMA

"The first entry point for all meditators is to investigate your own mind. This is the supreme and unequalled instruction."

The Place Where the Buddha Was Enlightened

First, you need to prepare a good cushion that is appropriate for practicing meditation.

A long time ago our Teacher the Buddha decided to search for a place to become awakened at the Bodhimanda, the Heart of Enlightenment.

When he sat near a large rock and flowering fruit tree, the gods encouraged him to travel to the west bank of the river Nairanjana, to Vajrasana, the Diamond Throne. He traveled there using ten types of meditative absorption and fifty-four special powers. When he arrived at the diamond-like mountain peak, he was blessed by the Buddhas of this Fortunate Era.

The Bodhi Tree, the Tree of Enlightenment, which is made from seven precious substances, appeared before him. It was surrounded by indications of the place's auspicious virtue, such as meadows of miraculous lotus blossoms.

The Buddha knew that the Buddhas of the past had sat on a seat of grass. No sooner had he thought this, than Indra understood his mind, and gathered from the Fragrant Mountains grass that felt as soft as cotton. Indra appeared in the form of Svastika the grass merchant and offered the grass to the Buddha.

Then the Buddha said,

Svastika has offered the grass to me.
Today this grass is so important to me.

I will overcome the demon Mara and his troops.
And feel the holy peace of enlightenment.

He infused the grass with truth so that it became full of
life. Then he arranged the grass into a seat with the tips of
each stalk facing inward. He sat down, and spoke these
words from the *Scripture of the Great Game*,

Though my body may wither on this seat, fine.
Though skin, bones, and flesh break down, fine.
Until I reach the highest enlightenment (so difficult to gain)
I shall not move from this seat.

And as he made this vow, the six great worlds rumbled.
The gods of the good came to his aid. The Buddhas and their
spiritual heirs spoke words of truth to him. In the evening the
Buddha tamed the demon Mara. Through the night he stayed
in meditative absorption. And at dawn he became truly and
totally enlightened.

These stories must be integrated into the practice of disciples who follow the life and liberation of the Buddha.

The Grass Seat

Sometimes it said that one should draw an image of a vajra
or an auspicious cross on the place where one is sitting. But
this falls under the fault of stepping on the name of a god, so
it is not appropriate to do this on a meditation seat. And
drawing an auspicious cross all over with white chalk is both
a Buddhist and a Bon practice. The best thing for Buddhists
is therefore to draw a dharma wheel.

On top of that place kusha grass for the grass mat. Kusha
grass has buds and flowers. It is orderly, with many distinct
shoots coming out of one reed. It is a distinctive substance
that clears away all impurities, all faults. During prepara-
tions for permission ceremonies in esoteric practice, those
who have overcome faults gather kusha grass for use as a seat
or a cushion.

Students, begin laying the kusha grass down by reciting a mantra. Use the seed syllable Hum, which holds the mind of the Buddha with its five wisdoms, and the seed syllable Dhih, which holds learned wisdom, to recite over the grass. Place a cushion of this grass under the seat. Therefore, the disciple will be able to rely upon a purified substance for a seat, and disciples' minds will remain untroubled.

So, arrange some of that kusha grass, which has many good qualities from the ritually purified substances, with its tips facing inward. A carpet that is suitable to place on top of that will form a fresh seat even if you use it a long time, according to the twelve rules for ascetic practice. So that the damp floor does not create conditions for disease, place it on a bench with a latticework seat to make it higher. This should not be so high that it will cause one to fall from the seat. A bench of three and half to four and a half feet wide is good.

Meditation Posture

A text on Great Seal meditation says, "Take up the seven-point posture upon a platform that is good for concentration." So, prepare a four-sided seat that is appropriate for meditation. To achieve positive results during productive periods of meditation, the back of the seat should be somewhat elevated.

The qualified novice or full monk should sit upon that seat and assume the seven-point posture of Vairocana. Let your speech and your breath settle into a restful state. Bring some motivating thoughts to mind.

Now, at first you may ask if there are any quotes from scripture that are the sources of this practice. Master Kamalashila explains this in his three *Stages of Meditation*: "In the *Ground of the Listeners*, Master Asanga quotes the *Questions of Revata Scripture*: 'You may be in a monastery, you may be in the forest, you may be a householder. Wash your feet, sit cross-legged on a small or large platform, upon kusha grass. Keep your body erect and maintain mindfulness.'"

The Wensa Oral Tradition explains, "There are eight features of the Vairocana posture: (1) feet; (2) hands; (3) back; (4) the joining of teeth, lips, and tongue; (5) head; (6) eyes; (7) neck; and (8) breath."

Further Instructions for Tantric Meditation

These eight features are described in the following. [But first, if one is practicing the tantra contemplations of the Six Yogas of Naropa, know this:] All subtle and coarse karmic wind-energy carries conceptual thought, which distinguishes subject and object. This wind-energy moves along the left and right channels of the subtle body. To combine it within the subtle body's central channel, sit in the vajra posture, either with the right foot up as in the Father Tantras or the left foot up as in the Mother Tantras.

Now, first do vase breathing or the recitation of vajra syllables. In these practices the wind-energies enter, abide, and dissolve into the subtle body's central channel, which then penetrates the center of the energy nexus at the navel. In reliance upon these and other practices, both pure and impure illusory bodies are established.

The main cause of the illusory body is the fivefold luminosity, or rather the life-supporting subtle energy upon which luminosity is carried. According to both Father and Mother Tantras, the appearing illusory body and the empty clear light display energy.

In accordance with this, one should form a meditation mudra, or hand gesture. In this mudra the right hand is placed above the left according to Father Tantras, while the left hand is placed above the right hand according to Mother Tantras.

When you are practicing the stages of the path, put your right hand on top of your left, with both hands in a meditation mudra (just like you do in a ritual). Set your hands straight, about four finger widths below the navel. The *Root Tantra of the Secret Assembly* says,

There is no thing, so there is no meditator.
There is nothing to meditate upon, so there is no meditation.
There is no thing, there is no non-thing,
So there is nothing called meditation.

So put the tips of your thumbs together. This illustrates that the significance of this teaching from the *Secret Assembly* integrates with the spiritual path when the three doors to liberation open to their culmination.

Meditation Posture in Detail

Spine

Make your spine as straight as an arrow so that the twenty-one vertebrae of the spine are stacked like golden coins. This allows the gross and subtle wind-energies to be easily controlled.

Mouth

When you have purified all defects of your speech through chanting mantras, and established a stable concentration, it may be that saliva drips. To avoid this, place your teeth and lips together naturally, and place the tip of your tongue so that it just touches your palate.

Neck

The *Four Medical Tantras* explain that the first vertebra is the hidden space of wind-energy, the sixth for the heart, and the seventh for vital energy. Taking this into account, tilting your neck too much can impede the vital energy, so refrain from this. Bow your head slightly so that, when singing praises, you don't give rise to certain types of excitement, such as arrogance, desire, etc.

Eyes

The wind-energy is a vehicle of the five senses. The senses cannot go unchecked, nor should you give in to lethargy, such as being drowsy with sleep. To counteract these, keep your eyes open partially, place your gaze so that you can just see the right and left sides of your nose.

Arms

To enhance the aforementioned physical postures, settle both arms evenly, and set your shoulders like wings.

❀ ❀ ❀ ❀ ❀

These seven points of physical posture are profound exercises that are appropriate for both exoteric and esoteric traditions of sutra and tantra.

Marpa the Great Translator boasted, "You may collect all the practice instructions of Tibet, but there is not sitting practice that compares with mine, Marpa Lotsawa's." So it is true that you should practice with this physical posture. For if you do not, you will experience pain.

There are many ways that the characteristics and proper recollection of each point of this posture relate to the oral instructions on contemplative experience within the esoteric traditions. I will not discuss these here any further.

Exoteric texts such as the *Stages of Meditation* or *The Ground of the Hearers* teach the easy development of mental pliancy, ability to sit for long periods of time without experiencing physical fatigue. This practice tradition is distinct from non-Buddhist traditions. It produces faith in anyone who happens to see people practicing it. Considered to have great benefits, it was first taught by the Buddha and later by his spiritual descendants.

Breathing

Breath. The Wensa Oral Tradition adds breath to the list of seven physical postures. Through the left nostril, exhale all conceptual thought evolving from the three poisons (greed, hatred, and ignorance).

While practicing calm meditation, if your desire predominates, contemplate unpleasant things. When your hatred predominates, contemplate kindness. When dullness predominates, contemplate the twelve moments of interdependent arising. When arrogance predominates, contemplate the dividing of the elements. When conceptual thought predominates, contemplate the inhalation and exhalation of your breath.

Do not breathe through your nose such that it makes a huffing noise or a thumping sound. Exhale gently without taking special notice of exhalation and inhalation. Focus in this way for seven breaths, or twenty-one, or even one hundred.

When you settle the mind through this practice, the vital wind that carries unvirtuous conceptual thought dissipates, and negative delusions become quiet of their own accord. The radiant nature of the mind, which itself is ethically neutral awareness, vividly shines. With such a practice it becomes easy to focus on virtue and enact it.

Alternative Postures

You should sit in a posture that is agreeable to you. For some it is not possible to observe the full lotus position for an entire meditation session. In this case one can start out in that posture, and later move to either the half-lotus position, or the bodhisattva position, where one foot is in front of the other. There are many types of people. So, in the scriptures on monastic conduct, the Buddha said to Gavampati, one of his five close disciples, that it would be easy for him to cultivate meditative absorption while lying down. So even lying down should not prove to be an obstacle to engaging in contemplation.

Motivation for Meditation: Using Mind to Look at Mind

Master Tsongkhapa speaks of improving one's motivation for meditation:

> If you do not clear the darkness of extreme perspectives, which either reifies or negates phenomena, you will not behold the sun of reality's radiance. If you do not seek a jewel of a mentor

who is experienced in learning, reflection, and meditation, then even if you are a great meditator who practices day and night, you may rise to become a thoughtless demigod or may fall to become a beast. I cannot bear this, so I shall say a little. If there are errors, please bear with me.

Now, some authentic meditators who claim to follow the Great Seal or the Great Perfection tradition say they follow a method of calm and insight meditation that is taught in authentic exoteric and esoteric scriptures. They hold non-conceptuality to be the essence of meditation. A consequence of this is that they confuse meditation with post-meditation; they claim that in post-meditation any constructed phenomena whatsoever that appears, at any moment, is automatically liberated. Because of this they ignore all sources of virtue.

By contrast, Tsongkhapa instructed his disciples with a series of perceptive questions in *The Pure Intention*:

> Whatever type object you meditate upon, separate the time into two periods: the meditation itself and post-meditation break time. During meditation, meditate on the appropriate object. During break time, focus on virtuous behavior. If you practice in this way, your break time will enhance your meditation. How do you dedicate activities to virtue? How long should each meditation session be? And how many should you do? The beginning of meditations should be performed just like "In the Language of India," [which is said at the beginning of Indian Buddhist classics].

Let's begin to look at this more closely. Panchen Losang Chögyen taught according to these instructions of Master Tsongkhapa. He expanded Tsongkhapa's cloud of offerings for accomplishing meditative experience and realization. In his *Laughing Song of Losang: Questions and Answers*, he writes:

> The first entry point for all meditators is to investigate your own mind. This is the supreme and unequalled instruction.

The titles of Indian sutras, tantras, and treatises all start by saying "In the Language of India." Just so, it is important to investigate your mind at the beginning of whatever you are doing—learning, reflecting, or meditating.

In the case of meditation, our primary mind is by nature neutral. A component of that neutral mind is a quick, subtle, and clear watchful awareness. Use this to investigate how that more general state of mind is doing, how it is thinking.

Motivation for Meditation:
The Need to Develop a Meditation Practice

Why? Because for as long as we thoughtlessly wander through these cycles of existence, we and every other living being throughout time desires to soothe the suffering that we experience in our own minds. And we desire to achieve happiness. We consider these desires to be burdens that are natural and inevitable.

Up to this point we have not attained the state of an enlightened being. Yet nevertheless, now is the time we must take the first step upon whatever path is right for us among the three ways—Theravada, the Way of the Elders; Mahayana, the Great Way; or Vajrayana, the Diamond Way. As long as that does not happen, we remain overpowered by our own thoughts. Our minds are under the sway of endless and varied negative emotions. Because of this, our minds are obscured by dense and dark clouds formed out of the habits that result from the accumulation of negative actions that we have failed to reckon with.

Because of this, everything we think and do turns out wrong. At the very least, we worry in our innermost heart that we cannot even have confidence that we won't be born into negative circumstances. Seeing that we cannot be free from the grip of this worry, we cling to some permanence in the happiness of the false notion that it is possible to avoid sorrow and depression amidst the things of this cyclic existence, if only for a moment. And when we do this, we naturally engage in behaviors that only serve to deepen this ocean of suffering. So tragic that we engage in such behavior!

For this reason, Master Tsongkhapa states in his *Pure Intention*:

> In a quiet place, set your body in the correct posture, and face your mind inward, thinking right thoughts. Start by cultivating a vivid feeling:
>
> "Since time immemorial I have endured the pain of suffering upon this deep bed of cyclic existence. We have experienced this due to our own minds. Starting today, I must do whatever I can to prevent being reborn in circumstances such as these. If I don't work toward this, my resilience will fail."

Cultivate this thought so that it feels as intense as an acute pain in your kidney. Such a thing is very difficult. Yet if we do not cultivate experience in this, even if a spiritual master teaches the profound means for liberating oneself from cyclic existence, and even if we learn this teaching, it's like water that is frozen on the surface. If you are not thirsty, for instance, then you won't look for a way to drink the water below. If you consider this carefully, you will see that this is true.

We must properly prepare our minds against moral downfall with mindfulness and conscientiousness. If we do not develop such genuine spiritual practice, even animals are better than us humans, inasmuch as they are better at gathering food. If you investigate the teachings of the founding figures of the Kadam tradition, this will become clear.

So each of us has attained a human body. Yet we do not realize that we are already stricken with existential illness, so we fall into error. This is like a person who is not in their right mind and does exactly the opposite of what the doctor prescribes.

And it is not just us who does this: nearly everyone who lives in this cyclic existence—who have each been at one time your mother—fails to give even a moment's notice to the profound teachings that can free them from these negative states. So, from this moment onward, we must not engage in activities that prevent us from making an effort. If we do not do so now, what hope is there that we will ever have such excellent human physical existence again? Even if you got lucky once and attained such a good human existence, it could be cut short in just a moment. This is simply the reality of impermanence. So, bring to mind a clear sense of how sad it is that, just as you wander in this cyclic existence, which is nothing more than an impermanent state, so, too, do all living beings.

CHAPTER THREE

LIVING AND DYING

INTRODUCTION

"'This human life, a foundation for freedom, is so valuable. It is hard to gain a life like this again! I reflect upon this holy instruction again and again. Contemplating this I encourage myself to make something of this life.'"

This chapter introduces what are perhaps the most popular set of contemplations on the unique opportunities and the considerable challenges of being human in Tibetan Buddhism: the "foundation practices." Foundation practices orient the contemplative practitioner to fundamental Buddhist ways of understanding human existence. The practices ask us to consider the simultaneous joy and sorrow, pleasure and pain, satisfaction and disappointment that constitute the shifting range of reactions to physical, personal, interpersonal, and environmental experiences. In the process of singling out both the opportunities and costs of life, as well as practices that, ideally, might shift the balance of our experience from dissatisfaction to contentment, those who undertake these foundational activities become better trained to engage in meditation in terms of motivation, endurance, and mental flexibility.

Sometimes these routines are called "preliminary practices" or "introductory practices" because they are intended as training for more intensive and complex forms of meditation, including visualization and imaginative manipulation of what Buddhism identifies as subtle yet powerful energies coursing through the body—practices on which the Thirteenth Dalai Lama briefly spoke in the preceding chapter. Yet Buddhist teachers stress that serious and sustained consideration of the spiritual exercises presented here is a lifelong pursuit. They are foundational in the sense that they form the basis of a specifically Buddhist contemplative approach to meditation, and to life more generally. And this foundation benefits from continual improvement, maintenance, and repair.

The foundation practices are a series of contemplations, or perhaps thought experiments, that are shared by all traditions of Tibetan Buddhism. There are a fixed number of practices, though the number and order vary across traditions, and even among writers in the same tradition. Typically, there are eight, nine, or twelve foundation practices. These are divided into a first set referred to as "common" practices, and a second set of "uncommon" practices. The common preliminary practices are shared across the major forms of Indian and Tibetan Buddhism. The ideas and practices in this set are common to Buddhism—the value of human existence, ethical cause and effect, the ubiquity of suffering, and the possibility of freedom.

The uncommon preliminaries are the distinctive contribution of Tantric Buddhism, which makes extensive use of the body as a vehicle for developing new patterns of thought and expanding positive emotions. These practices include ritual offerings, full prostrations of devotion, and chanting phrases—mantras—in order to purify and strengthen one's capacity to practice meditation. Often these rituals, prostrations, and chants are repeated many times per day over a period of many days. Some traditions mandate that practitioners perform one hundred thousand each of these in the context of a three-year meditation retreat. The work presented here focuses on the common foundation practices; the uncommon practices may be found in books in the Suggestions for Further Reading section.

This chapter is an excerpt from an eighteenth-century instruction on the foundation practices, entitled *The Source of All Attainment: An Essential Summary of the Stages of the Path to*

Enlightenment. This text presents the foundation practices in the context of a larger program of spiritual exercise called "stages of the path to enlightenment," a formal way of presenting a complete plan of Buddhist thought and practice that was popular within the Geluk School of Tibetan Buddhism.

Whether presented as a freestanding set of foundation practices, or embedded within a more extensive system such as the stages of the path to enlightenment, these exercises share a common narrative blueprint for spiritual practice, which goes something like this:

Being a human is, above all, a singular opportunity to develop oneself spiritually—and specifically to learn how to be benevolent to others. Buddhist practitioners should take advantage of this opportunity to reduce suffering for oneself and others. For the only constant in life is change. Humans tend not see it this way, so they crave permanence, and they suffer because of this. Developing a felt sense of the pervasive nature of change makes people happier because they loosen their compulsive grip on that ever-elusive dream, permanence. What's more, there is no place in which beings do not experience suffering. Gods suffer. So do animals. Abysmal states of existence, symbolized by the hell realms, are hot, cramped, and profoundly painful. The suffering that living beings experience in abysmal states, and in every other state of existence, is created by negative karma—ethical cause and effect—which humans engage in because they do not correctly relate to the one constant of life: change.

The Source of All Attainment was written by the principal tutor to the Eighth Dalai Lama, a prolific scholar and experienced contemplative from the Geluk School named Yeshé Gyeltsen (1713–1793). Although this scholar taught one of the most important Tibetan Buddhist leaders alive in the eighteenth century, he spent much of his time at a retreat center in the forests of southwestern Tibet. The weather and the landscape in this region are more forgiving than the high plains of central Tibet, where his famous student spent his time, and it is no wonder that Yeshé Gyeltsen preferred to stay far away from the bustle of Lhasa and the Dalai Lama's court when he could. He wrote *The Source of All Attainment* at Tashi Samten Ling, his hermitage in the Kyirong region of southwest Tibet, an ideal forest setting to spend time reflecting on the opportunities and limitations of this life.

Yeshé Gyeltsen offers brief contemplative exercises for seven foundation practices: (1) the unique opportunity of human life; (2) contemplating death and impermanence; (3) contemplating the sufferings of abysmal states of existence; (4) contemplating refuge in the Buddha, the dharma, and the Buddhist community; (5) contemplating karma, or ethical cause and effect; (6) contemplating freedom from compulsive behavior; and (7) contemplating the reversal of self-cherishing. Each of these contemplations takes the form of a self-dialogue, in which the practitioner spells out for oneself a basic Buddhist perspective on life as well as potential ways to reorient oneself toward more healthy ways of being in the world. Each takes place, in a Buddhist context, with supportive presence of one's teacher, or perhaps the Buddhist deity one chooses to represent one's particular strengths in spiritual matters: "Imagining your mentor deity at the crown of your head, contemplate the following . . ." the text instructs, indicating that one is never alone, never separate from the Buddhist masters of the past, or the timeless Buddhist spiritual forces, that provide support to those working on building a solid existential and emotional framework—a foundation—for meditation practice.

THE SOURCE OF ALL ATTAINMENT, BY YESHÉ GYELTSEN

The Unique Opportunity of a Human Life

Imagining your mentor deity at the crown of your head, contemplate the following:

"This human life, a foundation for freedom, is so valuable. It is hard to gain a life like this again! I reflect upon this holy instruction again and again. Contemplating this I encourage myself to make something of this life.

"For ages I have wandered through the material, the immaterial, and the yearning worlds. Long have I wandered through cyclic existence with no rest or ease, mainly drifting through a dreary land devoid of possibility. I did not encounter essential teachings such as those of the Buddha.

"Yet now I am fortunate. Through the strength of my mentor's compassion I have achieved a human body. With this good foundation I can certainly achieve an excellent pathway toward superior conditions, toward liberation."

❉   ❉   ❉   ❉   ❉

"So I will not meaninglessly squander this foundation for freedom, this human life that is more valuable than any wish-granting jewel. I must seize the heart of it, which is so great with purpose. So I make an effort on this path to enlightenment, and pray for blessings that I may so do.

"If I do not seize the heart of this foundation for freedom, it will be so difficult to regain a life like this. I look at all the living beings in abysmal states of existence and know that obtaining a healthy human body is as rare as a daytime star. Being a healthy human who is capable of developing oneself in accordance with spiritual teachings is even more rare than the udumbara blossom. And actually achieving the preconditions for the freedoms and advantages is rarer still!

"This is quite clear if I examine the trajectory of my own life. I might return from a land of the wish-granting jewels empty-handed. Just so, if I do not practice spiritual teachings while I possess both freedom and advantage, I'll fall into an abysmal state of existence. It's too bad that people delude and deceive themselves about this!

"The business of this life is like a children's game, or the dramatic act of a madman. I shall not crave it. I will focus intensely on the vital heart of life, the path to enlightenment, and I will make great effort. I pray for blessings that I may be able to do so."

Three Capacities

There are three ways of seizing the heart of life. These are each a way of cultivating the mind, each one of the three stages of the path to enlightenment: one for those with initial capacity, one for those with moderate capacity, and one for those with high capacity.

Contemplating Death and Impermanence

There are four contemplations for those with initial capacity. The first is meditation upon death and impermanence.

Imagining your mentor deity at the crown of your head, contemplate the following:

"Inappropriate action with body, speech, and mind, of whatever sort, is caused by a faulty mode of thinking that takes all objects to be permanent. The way to cultivate virtue for future states of existence is to be mindful of impermanence.

"All created things are transient, that is a common truth. Yet I especially may quickly die! I reflect on this day and night and urge myself to practice this excellent path.

"This foundation for freedom, so valuable, so difficult to achieve, will not survive long. It will quickly come to ruin. A rock falling from atop a tall cliff might strike me, and in an instant bring my comfort and ease to an end. So there is no place on earth where the lord of death cannot seize me. Foods, medicines, sheer might—none of these can turn back the lord of death.

"Even at times when we are only somewhat healthy, sleep, idle chatter, food, and drink as well as other meaningless activities distract us, and we don't have the chance to reflect on spiritual teachings. Even the holy ones display passing from life, so how is it that a little bubble of a body like me won't die?

"So I must reflect upon the reality of death and practice virtue day and night.

"I pray for blessings that I may be able to do so."

❀ ❀ ❀ ❀ ❀

"Not only will I die, but I have no way of knowing when I will die. The causes of death are so many, the causes of living so few. Most people will die unexpectedly. I am like a bubble upon the water, with a body weak and small. There is no assurance that I will not die this very day!

"Right now could be the moment when I die. So I will not be idle. I will not wait patiently. I shall strive to act virtuously every single moment. I pray for blessings that I may be able to do so.

"When I die nothing will be of any benefit, save spiritual teachings. People in this world—my family, my friends—may gather round me, but how does that benefit me at the moment of my death?

"I may hold glory and power over a billion worlds, yet there would not be even an atom that I could take with me to the next life. Even this body, which I protect and care for so dearly, will fall to ruin when the lord of death comes. Truly, it will be but an illusion.

"As I go toward the next life state, my Buddhist mentor, the Buddha, his community, and his teachings never lead me astray. The Buddhist spiritual teachings are of certain benefit. So, as I move toward the next state of life, I shall work with singular intent to practice the essence of the teachings on the path to enlightenment.

"I pray for blessings that I may be able to do so."

Contemplating the Sufferings of Abysmal States of Existence

Then there is a meditation on the sufferings of abysmal states of existence. Imagining your mentor deity at the crown of your head, contemplate the following:

"At the moment when I am bereft of this body, this foundation, I have no influence over where I am reborn. I must take rebirth under the influence of karma, ethical cause and effect.

"Where will the winds of negative karma carry me? This negative karma that I have accumulated since time immemorial is immeasurable, beyond number. And each minor unwholesome action, be it a thought such as the afflicting emotions or the three poisons of greed, hatred, and ignorance, or an action such as the behavior from negative karma, is said to be exponentially experienced in subsequent states of life.

"So if I wish to block the entrance through which I emerge in abysmal states of life, I shall work hard to abandon sin and cultivate virtue.

"I pray for blessings that I may be able to do so."

❁ ❁ ❁ ❁ ❁

"Right now I cannot bear to be so much as even touched by flame. How would it feel to experience my whole body burning in molten metal atop a blazing iron griddle? I shudder just hearing about it, not to speak of actually seeing it!

"If right now I cannot bear even a moment of freezing cold, if blizzard ice were to cleave my body into a hundred pieces and my body were to be racked with painful cold, who would protect me?

"If right now I cannot stand to go a single night without food, were I to become a hungry ghost who has not even heard the word *food* for a century, what would I do? Right now I am powerless to avoid being born into these states.

"If right now I cannot bear even a single harsh word, were I to become a poor, helpless animal who is beat, bound, sliced, and slaughtered, who would there be to protect me?

"Right now, in this moment when I have autonomy, were I not to block the entrance through which I emerge into abysmal life states, there is no doubt that I will lose my mind. So I shall work hard to abandon sin and cultivate virtue.

"I pray for blessings that I may be able to do so."

Contemplating Refuge in the Buddha, the Dharma, and the Buddhist Community

Now, there is a way to experience refuge. Imagining your mentor deity at the crown of your head, contemplate the following:

"If I cannot bear the sufferings of abysmal life states, I shall take refuge deep down in my bones in the singular refuge that protects from that abyss, the infallible mentor and the three jewels: the Buddha, his teachings, and the Buddhist community.

"Other than reliance upon the source of refuge, the three jewels, no living being in any realm of existence enjoys protection from the abysmal life states within this cycle of existence. For the noose of negative karma and afflictive emotions binds us all.

"Even if the compassion of the three jewels is great, if I do not personally have confidence in them, they are not able to protect me. The hook of death might be sharp and well cast, but it still can't catch a round stone!

"So I shall continuously contemplate the unfathomably good qualities of the three precious jewels, and with heartfelt faith and confidence I will cultivate trust, conviction, and determination."

❀ ❀ ❀ ❀ ❀

"I bring to mind the body of the Buddha. I hear the Buddha's melodious teachings in my ears. I have confidence when I ask for the Buddha's compassion. And because of this I know that I will certainly be liberated from abysmal states of life even when I find myself emerging in them. The Buddha speaks with a voice inerrant and true.

"I am terrified that I will come to be in abysmal states of life, though I have single-pointed faithful confidence that the three jewels will guard me from abysmal life states. It is said that this is essence of experiencing refuge.

"I pray for blessings that I may be able to do so."

A Refuge Prayer

These are the foundations of refuge. Now, the practice of refuge is like this:

I and all mothers, fathers, and living beings,
  Seek refuge in the three jewels.
  Care for us with your compassion.
  Protect us now from the terrors of life and death.

Recite this as many times as you like.

Contemplating the Refuge Precepts

Here is what you should do to study refuge precepts:

"I seek refuge in the three jewels with all my heart. I must practice according to their words, so I will protect the refuge precepts more dearly than life itself.

"I pray for blessings that I may be able to do so.

"I take the teacher, the Buddha as my refuge, without taking other worldly deities as refuge.

"No matter what my statue of Buddha may look like, I will not address him with disrespect, and I will pray to him with head bowed low.

"I have taken the spiritual teachings as my refuge, so I shall not place trust in those that are not this. No matter how un-polished the letters on the page are, I will not treat them with irreverence and disrespect, and I will pray to them with head bowed low.

"I have taken refuge in the noble community, so I shall not spend time with harmful acquaintances who maintain a nega-tive outlook. I take Buddhist monastics of all levels of vows to be sources of merit, and I faithfully pray to them."

❀ ❀ ❀ ❀ ❀

"When I take heartfelt refuge in the three jewels, positive qual-ities from vows and the like develop. I won't be disturbed by harm from people or other beings. My aims, both mundane and ultimate, will be fulfilled. I am a part of the Buddhist community and protected by the Buddha and his disciples as if I were their child.

"So I have confidence in the vast benefits of refuge, just as the Buddha taught. I take refuge at all times, morning, noon, and night. Whatever I do at any time, I do so paying homage to the three jewels. I shall not forsake the three jewels, even for my own life.

"I understand all joy and happiness to be the kindness of the three jewels, so I work hard to make offerings to them all of the time.

"I pray for blessings that I may be able to do so."

Contemplating Karma

Now, there is a meditation on the root of all goodness, namely confident faith in karma, or ethical cause and effect. Imagining your mentor deity at the crown of your head, contemplate the following:

"The root of all goodness is simply confident faith in cause and effect. The Buddha widely declared this in his majestic and melodic voice. So I shall contemplate both positive and negative ethical cause and effect.

"The capacity to clarify moral decision-making in relation to positive and negative cause and effect and does not exist anywhere in the world save the Buddha's compassionate intelligence. So I shall cultivate conviction in the Buddha's words.

"The ground and the mountains may sail up into the heavens. The sun, moon, and stars may fall to the earth. Yet the Buddha will never utter a false word. So I shall acquire conviction in the Buddha's words.

"I may not want suffering, but it is produced through thirsting after immoral activity. Even if I want happiness, suffering is produced because I do not practice virtue.

"My moral decision-making is backward; I am deceiving myself! Contemplating ethical cause and effect, I shall avoid errant behavior and practice virtue.

"I pray for blessings that I may be able to do so."

✳ ✳ ✳ ✳ ✳

"Virtuous behavior produces happiness, and unvirtuous behavior produces suffering. If there is no cause accumulated, there will be no result. Causes that are accumulated are never lost. Errant behavior toward family and relations will result in negative results that I alone will experience. If I don't give a portion to another, I will have no portion. Minor positive and errant behaviors produce larger effects. If I degrade someone by saying, "You are like a monkey!" I may be a monkey in five hundred lives. For, as the Buddha says, the effects of karma are vast.

"So I will contemplate the ways of ethical cause and effect. I will monitor my body, speech, and mind at all times. With firm mindfulness I will abandon errant behavior and strive to practice virtuous behavior.

"I pray for blessings that I may be able to do so.

"And even though I make such an effort, I am controlled by afflictive emotions. Because of this, negative behaviors of body, speech, and mind arise, just like a poisonous snake appearing out of nowhere. But I will immediately purify them through confession.

"I pray for blessings that I may be able to do so."

The Need to Work on the Introductory Contemplations

These contemplations on relying on a spiritual friend, appreciating freedom and opportunity, and so forth, are for an introductory audience. They are the foundation, the root of all subsequent spiritual progress, so everyone should practice them sincerely.

You should scrutinize these topics again and again with as much intellectual effort as you can, and in relationship to scriptural teachings, spiritual instructions, and various modes of reasoning. Safeguard these practices, and you shall develop all sorts of contemplative experience.

If you do not make an effort in these foundational aspects of the spiritual path, then it won't matter how much effort you put in on any more advanced level or path; your contemplative experience will not extend beyond mere verbiage. This is said to be unstable, like building a house on a bed of ice.

If you make an effort in these foundations of the spiritual path, and gain some familiarity with contemplative experience, then you will easily cultivate the higher qualities. Using that experience as a basis, the Buddha has said that liberation will come about.

Indications That You Have Made Progress

Indications that you have cultivated contemplative experience regarding the introductory practices include:

Before, you involuntarily thought only of this current life. Future lifeworlds were no more than fleeting words to you. Now that you have made extensive and enduring effort in these contemplations, you are mindful only of future lifeworlds. This lifeworld has become but a fleeting thing for you. Once you have cultivated thoughts such as these, you must continuously extend and nurture them. This is what the Buddha taught.

Contemplating Freedom from Compulsive Behavior

Within the standard stages of the spiritual path for intermediate audiences, there are two contemplations. The first of these is cultivating the wish to be free of compulsive ways of life.

Imagining your mentor deity at the crown of your head, contemplate the following:

"I know the nature of suffering in these realms of compulsive living. If I don't cultivate revulsion and remorse about this suffering, no matter what I do I will relive these compulsive modes over and over again. I must cultivate thoughts of pure renunciation.

"No matter where I might be born, from the most exalted life to the most terrible hell, suffering is the nature of life. For I am helplessly controlled by my negative ethical behavior and afflictive emotions, tightly bound and endlessly tortured by the three kinds of suffering.

"I experience birth, aging, illness, and unwanted death. I'm cut off from what I love. I don't get what I want. My negative behavior and afflictive emotions bind me within this mortal coil. These eight forms of suffering persecute me without interruption.

"All that I have amassed I will be separated from. All that I have collected will come to nothing. A high person must finally fall, and birth must end in death. People are my friends one moment and my enemies the next, so there is nothing in this compulsive existence in which I can place my trust.

"Sometimes the suffering strikes so fierce that I want to weep. People who think they are happy experience the suffering of change. And always these contrived thought and behavior patterns result in suffering. Never is there release from this prison cell of compulsive living.

"Grant me blessings that I may cultivate an intense wish for liberation."

Contemplating the Reversal of Self-Cherishing

When you come to understand the nature of this suffering and cultivate an intense wish for liberation, you will then need to seek means to liberate yourself from compulsive living. So here is how to train on the spiritual path to liberation.

Imagining your mentor deity at the crown of your head, contemplate the following:

"If I do not understand the seeds of existence, then even if I wish to avoid suffering, I will not be able, just like the root of the tree remains underground. I must cut the root of compulsive living.

"Since time immemorial a great demon of self-cherishing has resided deep in my heart, always thinking, 'Me! Me!' It severs self from other and creates emotional attachment and aversion. The negative causes and effects of this continually generate compulsive modes of living.

"I must reverse self-cherishing, the root of compulsive life, for which I need the eye of wisdom that understands its true reality. So I will clean my mind's eye with the elixir of meditation. And to keep this elixir of focused meditation, I shall need the vessel of ethics, for ethics is the root of all enlightened qualities. So I shall hold ethics to be dearer to me than my own life.

"I pray for blessings that I may be able to do so."

❀ ❀ ❀ ❀ ❀

After training with immense effort within the intermediate practices, how will progress in transforming your mind become apparent? Indications that you have cultivated contemplative experience regarding the intermediate practices include: You will experience deep sadness and revulsion toward all ways of life in these cycles of existence, just like a bird feels on a frozen lake. "I must escape from this ever-spinning prison!" you will think, and you will naturally develop a wish for spiritual freedom. This is what the Buddha taught.

CHAPTER FOUR

SONGS OF IMPERMANENCE

INTRODUCTION

Dharma Master Sun has set.
And so I've now become
A dark and dismal hue.
Rain tears ready
To fall upon my face.

Some Tibetan Buddhist texts on meditation read like manuals. This is a good thing; they tell us what to do, when to do it, and with what motivation. They even give us a script to recite, remember, or revisit when we are unclear how to proceed. Yeshé Gyeltsen's instructions on how to contemplate the unique opportunity that each of us has to practice meditation is a perfect example of a Buddhist manual. Each of the spiritual exercises in the previous chapter was clearly outlined: First, one imaginatively recalls one's teacher. Next, one rehearses the exercise itself, going through the basic Buddhist principles, one's own motivation to apply those principles to life. Finally, one requests help in successfully applying them by seeking the blessings of the teachers and potent spiritual beings of the Buddhist tradition. This is a manual for spiritual exercise.

Yet there are other ways of getting at the same issues. Poetry is one, perhaps the most important alternative means to evoke the contemplative life. We read Shabkar's poetry on mountain retreat and varieties of meditators in chapter 1; in this chapter we will hear from Shabkar on the pervasiveness of sorrow, dissatisfaction, loss, and frustration in human life. Thematically these poems are directly related to the second foundation practice in chapter 3: "contemplating death and impermanence." The inevitability of death and the stark reality of impermanence are key themes in Buddhism, and perhaps the most important motivators among the foundation practices. They instill, in an ideal Buddhist program of spiritual development, a sense of urgency to one's efforts.

What a poetic voice brings to the contemplation of death and impermanence is an expanded repertoire of resources for imagining impermanence in relation to the vivid details of our lived experience, and a nuanced tool for working through the often-intense emotions that arise when contemplating our own mortality. The prose of Yeshé Gyeltsen's instruction teaches, but the poetry of Shabkar's verse sings. And in singing about mortality, the songs lend us voice to express our own fears, our own longing, our distinctive feelings as we learn to be with life's transience.

This chapter presents six songs of spiritual experience dedicated to the themes of death and impermanence. Each offers something unique to the contemplative practitioner. "Death Will Give No Chance to Act" uses a repeating song form to evoke shifting feelings of sorrow, melancholy, or deep concern for the fate of living beings—concluding with ourselves. The song moves easily from image to image, scene to scene, landscape to landscape. Animals make up the central characters as each verse sketches a dramatic scene of life and death. In the end we see that the red buck of verse one and the gold-eyed fish of verse three are none other than ourselves, the meditator who had sought to spend time in mountain retreat but has waited too long to act.

"My Master Is Gone" is a brief and vivid example of a classic form, a song in remembrance of one's teacher. As is clear from the frame of each spiritual exercise in chapter 3, the spiritual mentor is a foundational figure of the Buddhist meditator's life. Without the mentor, the student would simply be unable to learn how to practice, how to cultivate the skills and the existential outlook that enable one to develop. Time and again Tibetan Buddhist texts on meditation stress the importance of the mentor, the person who walks one through the often-unspoken complexities of contemplative practice. The tradition is insistent that students take great care to honor the memory of their deceased teachers. Generations of songs in memory of mentors give voice to the deep, emotionally charged relationships that can grow between teacher and student. Shabkar's poem to his master condenses this rich emotional life into three verses, each a miniature scene of sorrow and longing.

As with the previous song, the two living beings in the first verses, lotus and cuckoo, are metaphors for the singer, reader, or reciter of the song, the disciple, looking back on the vital energy that their meditation master bequeathed before passing on. The next song continues the theme of memory and sadness. "Father Is Gone" also evokes one's teacher, though this time Shabkar's teacher is characterized as a parent, a father, with all the emotional charge that this carries. Here each verse guides one's memory to a certain aspect of the father/teacher's living presence—his look, his voice, his love, the way he acted when he was alive, when he was standing right before his student.

"I Am a Cloud" adopts a more playful tone. A significant ingredient in Shabkar's popularity as a poet-saint is his capacity to treat even the gravest topics in Buddhism with gentle wit, with a humor that offers lightness—"I am a cloud!"—even in the face of great sorrow.

"Fish, Sun, and Pomegranate" continues the playful, or perhaps absurdist, tone of the previous song, though this time focusing on the melancholy of having a friend depart to other ventures in life. The student, the "big faithful fish" has left the mountain hermitage, or perhaps the small regional monastery, and gone to the large center of learning, one of the huge monastic colleges that form the intellectual and institutional heart of Tibetan Buddhist culture. But there is danger in moving too far from the retreat center, from the natural place of meditators; will the student become caught up in competition inherent to institutional life? Will the once-faithful fish be snared by the fisherman's hook? Even in routine social relationships or institutional life there is human mortality, human frailty that merits contemplation as much as the more abstract notions of cyclic existence or impermanence.

Finally, "To Sing a Song Forever" offers a more hopeful perspective on impermanence. Rulers may rise and fall, mountains may crumble, heroes may pass from memory. Yet through all this the Buddhist teachings will endure so long as the Buddhist hermits maintain their contemplative practice. The meditator may be humble compared with rulers and heroes, no more than a beggar, yet their practice will endure. Here Shabkar turns from sorrow to hope, from melancholy to optimism, from a focus on death and impermanence to the profound opportunity that life presents, the possibility of enlightenment, of joy through the simple practice of meditation. Shabkar's song of forever, his reflective praise of the meditator's path, prepares us to return to more formal meditation in the next chapter.

Death Will Give No Chance to Act

A buck, dark red.
Youthful and strong,
The hunter kills him.
Just like that.

Left standing in his tracks,
A doe.
Don't flee downhill.
Just keep to ground.

When will the hunter come?
Don't know.
Keep to your hiding place always.

He comes.
And now you want to run.
But Hunter gives no chance to run.

A fish, gold-eyed.
Youthful and strong.
Fisherman kills him.
Just like that.

Left swimming in his wake,
Little fish.
Don't circle the shore.
Keep to the deep.

When will the fisherman come?
Don't know.
Keep to your hiding place always.

He comes. And now you seek escape.
Fisherman gives no chance to flee.

A friend, young.
In the prime of life.
Died suddenly.
Just like that.

Left in his path,
An old beggar,
Don't wander to town.
Keep to the hills.

When will the Death Lord come?
Don't know.
Practice the gods' faith always.

Death comes.
And now you long for faith.
But Death will give no chance to act.

My Master Is Gone

The sunlight breaks on land,
To set on mountains west.

It leaves a fragile lotus,
Cold and crushed by frost.

Summer cloud swells blue,
To fade into the sky.

It leaves a fragile cuckoo,
Racked by fearsome thirst.

My kindly master's gone,
Set out for other realms.

He leaves a frail pupil,
Depressed by signs of age.

Father Is Gone

Lake Heart, stunning.
Flowers bloom green blue.
I remember Father's look.

Carefree birds.
Shouting for joy.
I remember Father's voice.

Sky-wide heavens.
Cloudless and clear.
I remember Father's love.

Blue lake, spotless.
Shimmering, rippling.
I remember Father's way.

I Am a Cloud

Big-sky trails
Across the Snowy Land,
Brilliant white with joy.

I am a cloud!

Dharma Master Sun has set.
And so I've now become
A dark and dismal hue.

Rain tears ready
To fall upon my face.

Shifting shapeless,
Here, there, up and down.
Until ill winds of death
Break me apart.

At times the rain sprinkles.

At times it pours.

Fish, Sun, and Pomegranate

Gone, big faithful fish
Set out for the sea of scholars.
Religious currents
Flow where they will.

Be glad if jealousy's hook
Does not catch up with you.

Learning sun, thinking moon
Shine on the fortress of scripture.

Ignorant shadows
Gloomy, blot you out.

Be glad a wicked star
Does not catch up with you.

Holy dharma pomegranate,
Eaten when mature, so
Empty stomach Self
Is somewhat satisfied.

Be glad a teaching famine
Does not catch up with you.

To Sing a Song Forever

Now all the eagle kings
Have vanished into space.

Amidst the forest trees,
The bees still babble on.

Now all the grand rivers,
Have drained into the sea.

Amidst the river rocks,
The brook still babbles on.

Now bygone champions,
Have left for other realms.

Inside a barren cave,
The beggar babbles on.

Small, forgotten, and yet,
The buzz transcends the bee,

To hum the tune forever is,
The spirit of the bee.

Small, narrow, and yet,
The babble transcends the brook.

To babble on forever is,
The spirit of the brook.

Old, unwise, and yet,
Teachings transcend the man.

To sing a song forever is,
This old man beggar's way.

CHAPTER FIVE

INNER CALM

INTRODUCTION

"Calm meditation uses techniques for stabilizing the mind. It calms thoughts that fixate on characteristics of things and settles that stable mind within its own brilliant energy."

The most important type of basic meditation in Tibetan Buddhism is "calm meditation." In this practice contemplatives work to reduce the constant and often turbulent flow of thoughts and emotions that continuously courses through their minds. It is part of the essential training of the mind, and it is in this sense that we can call it a "basic" meditation. But it is a deep practice that can develop, expand, and nourish for a lifetime.

The mind is, as the translation presented in this chapter will detail, unruly when untrained, yet remarkably capable when trained. In fact, in the meditation traditions of Tibet, the mind is both the source of and the solution to the problem of suffering. The distinction between a wild animal and domesticated animal is sometimes used as a metaphor in the attempt to explain the vast difference between the untrained and the trained mind. A wild animal is powerful, yet it is unpredictable and potentially dangerous if one gets too close. So, too, the untrained mind; a mind that runs wherever its wild energies take it—the greed, hatred, and ignorance that Buddhism states lie at the heart of the untrained mind—is quite literally a danger to oneself and others. A tamed animal (an elephant is a favorite example in Buddhist literature) is still powerful, yet its energy can be channeled. It can be put to a purpose, deployed to create, to sustain, to move its human caretakers. So, too, the trained mind; a mind whose flexible capacity has been cultivated through meditation can do anything, from sorting out life's daily work challenges to carrying one on the path from ignorance and suffering to wisdom and joy. And the process of training the mind begins, in a formal sense, with calm meditation.

This presentation of calm meditation is from a sixteenth-century text called *The Ornament of the Three Visions* by Ngorchen Könchok Lhündrup (1497–1557). Our author was the abbot of the famous Ngor Monastery, which belongs to the Sakya School of Tibetan Buddhism. Like the Stages of the Path literature of the Geluk School, and the Great Seal foundation practice literature of the Kagyu School, the Three Visions literature of the Sakya School presents the introductory practices that form the foundation for further meditation. The "three visions" are: First, the impure vision of regular, unenlightened people. This is the state we all, Buddhism says, find ourselves within. We have less control of our thoughts, our emotions, our behavior, than we would like, and often (or nearly always, Buddhism would have it), we think, feel, and act in ways that are detrimental to ourselves and those around us—that is, unless we train our minds so that we can develop positive modes of thinking, feeling, behaving. Second, the "vision of experience" constitutes the habits of thought that a contemplative practitioner will, ideally, have cultivated through meditation practice and reflection upon Buddhist existential thought. This is the outlook of a dedicated trainee, well established in a contemplative practice. Third, finally, "pure vision" is the way of seeing and acting within the world that the Buddha and other enlightened beings dwell within. Pure vision is enlightenment itself. The Three Visions literature incorporates the foundation practices that we encountered in chapter 3. They also include insight meditation, which we will hear about in chapter 5, within their graded program of self-development from impure to pure vision.

The work presented in this chapter offers detailed yet concise instructions for beginning to calm the mind, for stabilizing that experience of calm once one has achieved it in some measure, and for finely adjusting one's delicate hold on the experience of a calm, stable mind as one learns to maintain it over ever-longer periods of time. A section-by-section overview of this relatively complex chapter will be helpful as one works through the succinct overviews of the practice's components.

"Preparing for Calm Meditation" emphasizes the need for solitude to practice calm meditation. This is solitude of body and mind. This text was intended for monastics who would dedicate themselves to the practice in a monastery or perhaps a nearby hermitage. Giving up worldly work, farming or trading, is a literal instruction for such an audience. But the larger purpose of solitude is solitude of the mind, which, *The Ornament of the Three Visions* tells us, means intentionally distancing oneself from objects of desire that are both material and conceptual. One must distance oneself from the constant effort to acquire ever more wealth, land, or material goods beyond the necessities of life. And one must distance oneself from immaterial commodities as well, such as fame, or influence, or even, more challengingly, relationships. (We will see in chapter 8, "Cosmic Love," that this does not always mean severing all relationships, but rather reframing relationships to include ever-expanding groups of human beings. In this sense, the call to give up relationships is a call to give up the partiality, the partisanship, that can come with relationships.) Yet though this text is meant for monks and nuns who would in reality head "up the mountain" to practice in meditation retreat, it also speaks to laypeople for whom "solitude" is as much a state of mind as it is a physical and social reality. Another way that *Three Visions* describes this is "nonattachment" to objects of desire, be they material or conceptual. Ngorchen Könchok Lhündrup quotes Buddhist scriptures and Indian Buddhist treatises to emphasize his point. The classic text known as *The Way of the Bodhisattva* is key here. This famous seventh-century Indian text, which covers

everything from ethics to ritual to spiritual exercises to philosophy, forms a basis for much of the Tibetan writing on
foundational Buddhist thought and practice we have encountered in the chapters up to this point, and it will make an appearance in later chapters as well.

Once one has gained for oneself a measure of solitude, of in-
tentional distance from the work and worries of the social and
economic realms, "Identifying and Learning to Correct Errors
in Calm Meditation" prepares the contemplative to begin calm
meditation. Here we are introduced to potential errors, habits
of thought and behavior that can hinder progress in meditation or prevent one from successfully beginning the process in
a meaningful way. These five faults are laziness, forgetfulness,
dullness and sluggishness, non-application, and overapplication. "Habits" is perhaps a better way to think of these than
"errors" or "faults," because in Buddhism any of these behavioral impediments can be corrected through training, through
self-development. Buddhism also has a discrete set of "antidotes," or methods of correcting these harmful habits.

"Calm Meditation: The Nine Placements of the Mind" begins the formal introduction to the practice itself. The nine
placements represent a gradual process of learning the meditation, familiarizing oneself with it through practice, stabilizing the capacity to calm the flow of thoughts and emotions
through sustained, diligent effort. Throughout this process
the practitioner gains increased experience of the lived intri-
cacy of turning one's consciousness in the direction of its
own workings. *Three Visions* offers brief definitions of each
one: (1) resting; (2) persistent resting; (3) correction and resting; (4) thoroughly resting; (5) pacifying; (6) calming; (7) full
calm; (8) focus; (9) resting in composure. These may seem
vague in the abstract, yet when coupled with advice for correcting calm, for shaping one's efforts to calm the mind, they
begin to emerge not as separate events but as a continuum of
mental work, where one "places" and replaces the mind again
and again until it begins to settle of its own accord.

As with any skilled practice, one moves from artificially
forcing the body or mind to go through the motions until it

begins to feel as if the body or mind were doing it "all by it-self." The nine placements attempt to capture something of this progress toward a "flow state" in which complex skills are so internalized that one does not distinguish between thinking about doing them and just doing them. As the ninth placement says, "Through making this habitual practice, you will not need to exert yourself in order for the mind to natu-rally become tranquil." "Correcting Laziness, Agitation in Calm Meditation" brings the first half of the text to a close by emphasizing the two greatest threats to successful calm meditation: laziness and mental agitation.

The next section, "Water Similes for Meditation Experi-ences," offers an extended simile for the moves that one's thoughts can make as one progresses through the nine steps of cultivating calm. It is notoriously difficult to describe con-sciousness in a way that does any justice to its vividness, its variability, and its depth. Buddhist meditation traditions start from the premise that most people are not well practiced in introspection. This makes a mental and physical program of self-development such as calm meditation challenging, espe-cially at the beginning, for it is often hard to ascertain with any degree of focus or confidence whether one's mind is calm or agitated in the first place! Similes such as water are key tools in the Buddhist contemplative tool kit to help practitio-ners assess themselves; if one cannot sufficiently name a cer-tain quality of mind, much less assign value to it, then perhaps an image such as the movement of water can offer a means to conceptualize something that is, ironically, so difficult to give a formal description of, such as the many ways that thought "moves" in us, through us—the ways it moves *us*. This sec-tion also names the experience that many novice meditators have when they first begin their practice, the feeling of having more thoughts than ever before. This is normal, *Three Visions* says. Do not worry. "These thoughts have been in your mind all along, but you have never recognized them because you have never composed your mind in contemplation," says Ngorchen Könchok Lhündrup. "Now that you are aware of them, you may think, 'I have more thoughts than ever!' or, 'I

am not meditating!' But this is the first experience of meditation. It is called 'like water rushing down a steep mountain.'"

The remaining five sections of the chapter briefly cover
more focused topics. "Cultivating Bright Clarity of Consciousness" compares the calmed mind to a candle flame that
is perfectly still, unmoved by any air currents. Mental "stillness" is a key result of calm meditation. Here *Three Visions*
introduces another feature of the mind when still, clarity
or "brightness." Buddhism likens the innate capacity of the
mind, its basic energy, to light, and the key evidence of this
is brightness. Other chapters will deepen this idea of mind in
its natural, undisturbed state as clear, bright, luminescent.
"Meditate in Good Health" emphasizes the fact that the mind
is part of the body. While traditional Buddhist texts do not
typically speak of the brain, they do point to the inextricable
relationship between body and mind. A healthy body is necessary for a healthy mind, and thus for the work of meditation.

"Contemplating the Significance of Meditation Practice"
provides a spiritual exercise much like those we have seen in
chapter 3. This is a guided self-dialogue on the importance of
calm meditation in the effort to achieve liberation from suffering. Like a candle blown by the wind, the mind is blown
about by the "winds" of cyclic existence.

"Investigating Your Emotions" offers more corrective measures as one deepens and improves one's capacity to calm the
mind, though this time with an emphasis on the emotions.
Are the feelings that come up harsh, or desirous? Or perhaps
jealousy or pride surges up during calm meditation. How
does one deal with the sudden upsurge of the very emotions
one is seeking to settle? *Three Visions* recommends a three-
pronged approach. First, take a breath: bring the mind back
into focus by counting your inhalation and exhalation. Second, ascertain the character of the emotion. Third, apply an
antidote based on what kind of emotion has emerged. This is
an ongoing process that can be done routinely during meditation sessions. "Refining the Corrective Measures in Meditation" offers assurance that the combination of direct calming
coupled with corrective techniques will result in a mind that

is both settled and focused. Over time, thoughts and emotions that once seemed to rule one's mind through chaos will settle. What will be left is the clarity, the clear energy of the experience of being aware. Focus, instructs *Three Visions*, on this clarity. Later chapters will expand upon this notion. Finally, "After the Meditation Session" urges the meditator to take a break, refresh one's body and mind, and to head back in for another session.

INTRODUCTION TO CALM AND INSIGHT MEDITATION

The means for cultivating an enlightened outlook are calm meditation and insight meditation.

Calm meditation uses techniques for stabilizing the mind. It calms thoughts that fixate on characteristics of things and settles that stable mind within its own brilliant energy.

Insight meditation removes the obscuring veil of dualistic thinking and differentiates the nature of things from their characteristics. It enables the meditator to view the natural face of the ever-present mind.

The *Cloud of Jewels Scripture* says, "What is calm meditation? It is a focused mind. What is insight meditation? It is discernment." The *Ornament for Scripture* says, "When mind is truly stable, and mind is settled within mind, and when this mind completely analyzes all things, this is calm and insight meditation."

There are three ways to practice these techniques: calm meditation, insight meditation, and the combination of the two. On these *The Way of the Bodhisattva* says, "It is known that insight meditation integrated with calm meditation overcomes afflictive emotions. So first you must seek calm meditation and based upon that you should happily practice nonattachment to the world."

So you need insight meditation to uproot the afflictive emotion of self-fixation. And in order to cultivate insight meditation, you need calm meditation.

Preparing for Calm Meditation

Calm meditation depends upon the solitude of both body and mind. So the first thing to do is give up the work of the world, such as agriculture or business. Then you must give up thoughts of desirable material objects, or interior desires such as longing for other people. If you do not give these up, you will not be able to develop a genuine meditation practice in which you are mentally focused.

The faults of being attached to the activity of the world is described in the *Scripture That Encourages Pure Intention*: "If the master encourages you, you are displeased. If the master teaches you to follow, you don't take this up willingly. Such actions quickly lead to poor conduct and are the result of attachment to the work of the world. Householders constantly think about making a living, so they are always distressed. Householders can neither concentrate nor give up the work of the world. This bad situation is caused by being attached to the work of the world."

The faults of desiring material objects are described in *The Way of the Bodhisattva*: "Desire produces destruction in this life and in the next. In this life you may be killed, or bound up, or maimed. In the next life you may experience a hellish existence." Recall also what *The Way of the Bodhisattva* says elsewhere: "Know that wealth is endlessly damaging. To amass it, to defend it, to lose it—all this is torment. People who are bound by desire for wealth have no chance to find release from the suffering of life."

The fault of being attached to other immature people is also described in the same text:

> If you are too attached to other people who are immature, your sense of reality becomes obscured. Your sorrowful thoughts worsen, and ultimately you are tormented with suffering. If your thoughts are exclusively determined by immature people, this life of yours passes by without purpose. Through fleeting acquaintances and relatives, even eternal spiritual teachings can deteriorate.

If you act like an immature person, you will without doubt meet with an awful fate. Why would you associate with immature people if this only results in an unfortunate outcome? One second, they may act like friends, and the next like enemies. They become angry in pleasant circumstances, so they are very difficult to satisfy. They are angered when you speak in a helpful way, and they steer you away from help. And when you fail to listen to what they say, they again become angry. This will lead them to an awful fate.

Immature people are jealous of superiors, competitive with peers, and arrogant toward people beneath them. They are stuck-up when praised, and furious when spoken to harshly. When do you ever reap any benefit from immature people? If you spend time with them, you come to act immature yourself, praising yourself, insulting others, or gabbing about the diversions of samsara. If you spend time with immature people, you will definitely become unvirtuous yourself.

The revered and esteemed Drakpa Gyeltsen also says, "Take up residence in a secluded place and develop your powers of concentration. If you spend time with immature people, you will not find a place of seclusion, so you should cultivate a feeling of disenchantment toward them. Through this you can find seclusion and abandon unhelpful ways of living."

You should also give up hateful thoughts toward your enemies. *The Way of the Bodhisattva* states, "If you cling to painful thoughts of hatred, your mind will never know calm. You will find no peace, no joy. You will not be able to sleep, and you will become unreliable. Those who venerate and reward a benevolent leader will just as well oppose and kill a hateful leader. Hatred brings sorrow to friends and relatives. Even if you gather them around you through giving them things, they will not be supportive toward you. In short, it is simply not possible to live happily through hatred." Beyond this, look to other passages in *The Way of the Bodhisattva* on the results of such activity.

In this way, give up all attachment to the things that you desire as well as the things that you hate. In isolated places such as a mountain valley or the forest, live by yourself and cultivate meditative stabilization (samadhi). *The Way of the Bodhisattva* says, "I shall live alone, all by myself. Content and happy in a bright and pleasant wilderness, with few cares, I will calm all distractions." And finally, it says, "Consider the good qualities of seclusion mentioned here. Cultivate the complete calming of your thoughts and cultivate an outlook that is focused on enlightenment.

Identifying and Learning to Correct Errors in Calm Meditation

When you are living in solitude and cultivating calm meditation, you must learn to recognize five errors, for these must be corrected. To do this you should rely on eight antidotes to these errors. The five errors are: laziness, in which you do not engage your mind in virtuous behavior; forgetfulness of the teachings on cultivating meditative concentration even if you do engage in virtuous behavior; dullness and sluggishness of mind even if you don't forget the teachings, or a murky restlessness of mind; not seeking out and applying the antidotes that will overcome the errors, even if you realize your mind has become dull or scattered; and the development of an unsettled mind through the overapplication of the antidotes. *Distinguishing the Middle from the Extremes* says, "Laziness, forgetfulness, dullness and sluggishness, no application, and overapplication: these are the five errors."

There are eight activities that correct the five errors. The first four, namely intention, perseverance, faith, and flexibility, are antidotes for correcting the first of the errors, laziness. Your intention is the state of meditative concentration. Perseverance is remaining in that state. Faith is what motivates your intention. Flexibility is a benefit developed from your perseverance.

The most important among these is perseverance. The meaning of perseverance is effort; this is what corrects laziness, so making an effort is very important. *The Way of the Bodhisattva* says, "You should practice effort by being patient. Enlightenment dwells in the effort. Just as there is no movement without wind, there is not merit without effort. What is effort? It is the love of virtue."

Factors that work against effort include the following: "Unproductive factors are laziness, desire for negative activities, procrastination, and self-loathing. Basking in the pleasures of lethargy, or longing only for sleep, you fail to mourn the sufferings of samsara, and you increase the error of laziness."

So you must counteract the causes of laziness. To do so, you should call to mind the faults of samsara, the difficulty in achieving a life of freedom and advantage, and the uncertainty of the moment of your death, and you should make a real effort to cultivate meditative concentration.

The antidotes to forgetting the contemplative instructions are remembering and paying attention. Whatever the central point of the instructions on cultivating meditative concentration are, you must remember them so that you keep them in mind. After this, pay attention so that you grasp those instructions without forgetting them.

The Way of the Bodhisattva says, "If you are afflicted by a lack of attentiveness, learning, contemplation, and meditation are like water poured into a leaky pot; they will not be retained in your memory."

The antidote to not recognizing dullness and agitation is to consciously recognize when you are under the control of either one, or when you are not. Both dullness and agitation are the primary factors that work against meditative concentration. So if you don't recognize them, you will not know how to rely on an antidote to them. And when you do recognize them but do not put in the work to dissipate your dullness or agitation, well then, the antidote is to do the work! For if you recognize what you need to correct yet fail to rely on the antidote, then you will not develop positive mental qualities.

If your thoughts have become too intense due to applying yourself too much, and will not settle down, the antidote is to balance your application of the practice. Just so, a wise person looks at their load of goods, measures it carefully in relation to a measure of gold, makes sure the two are even, and in this way easily achieves what they want.

Distinguishing the Middle from the Extremes says, "[You must understand] the state [of meditative concentration], how to dwell in that state, and both its causes and effects. [You must know how to] remember the key point of instruction, realize when you are dull or agitated working to correct them, and how to rest naturally in that state when you are calm."

Calm Meditation: The Nine Placements of the Mind

The specific steps to settle the mind are as follows: (1) resting; (2) persistent resting; (3) correction and resting; (4) thoroughly resting; (5) pacifying; (6) calming; (7) full calm; (8) focus; (9) resting in composure.

1. **Resting your mind:** The first of these nine is resting your mind. For this you need an object of meditation that is motionless. Your body should not stir. Your eyes should not blink much. The object of meditation should be clear.

The object of meditation that is motionless: In a place of deep solitude, you should place an object of attention, such as a beautiful painting of the Buddha, in a pleasing location. *The King of Meditative Concentration Scripture* says, "Whoever rests their mind upon the Buddha, the lovely golden-bodied Lord of the World, is a bodhisattva in meditative composure." Alternatively, place a blue flower, a piece of blue cloth, or whatever you have right in front of you. The object should be neither to far nor too close and should be motionless.

Your body should not stir: In the *Stages of Meditation* Kamalashila gives the following instructions. Your eyes should be pointed at the tip of your nose, without being wide open or fully closed. Keep your posture straight. Be mindful of your internal state. Your shoulders should be even. Your head should be neither too high nor too low and should form a line with your nose and navel without moving side to side. Keep your teeth and lips as they normally are and place your tongue at the base of your teeth. Your breath should flow in and out. It should not be audible, heavy, or aggressive. Rather you should inhale naturally in a relaxed manner so that you don't notice it at all. Your exhalation should be the same. Settle yourself on a comfortable seat in a full meditation posture, straight and motionless.

Your eyes should not blink much: Your eyelids should cover about half of your eyes. Look at the object of meditation without blinking. If tears come, let them fall without wiping them away with your hands. If you experience discomfort, do not set your mind upon it, but rather keep focused on the object of meditation and settle yourself.

The object of meditation should be clear: You should not place judgments upon the object of meditation. Do not judge it to be good or bad. Whatever features it may have should be placed clearly and lucidly within your awareness, without any preconceptions.

2. Persistent resting: In the beginning long periods of this type of meditation will not be possible. Therefore, persistently rest your mind again and again for short periods of time.

3. Correction and resting: If you waver, recognize this, and refresh your mind upon the object of meditation.

4. Thoroughly resting: To keep your mind from wandering, use mindfulness to remain right in front of the object of meditation.

5. Subduing: If your mind gets carried away in the good qualities of meditative trance and becomes either lazy or agitated, use correctives to subdue it.

6. Calming: If your mind becomes unhappy as a result of being distracted or some other reason, calm it by settling it on the object of meditation.

7. Persistent calming: If your mind develops thoughts that are opposed to meditative trance, such as envy, again calm the mind by remaining right in front of the object of meditation.

8. Focus: If you have performed methods to overcome laziness and agitation, yet your mind wanders, rest your mind on its own wandering.

9. Really resting in composure: Through making this habitual practice, you will not need to exert yourself for the mind to naturally become tranquil.

These techniques are the one-pointed calm meditation of our realm of reality, the Realm of Desire (the basic human experience). This calm meditation occurs prior to the development of highly cultivated forms of bliss. Only when this bliss is cultivated does the true calm meditation become complete, and this occurs at the Plateau of Meditative Trance (which we will not discuss here).

Correcting Laziness, Agitation in Calm Meditation

The *Ornament for the Sutras* says, "Set your mind on the object of meditation and do not let it waver. Quickly be aware when your mind does waver, refresh it, and set it on the object again. Wise people should bring their minds increasingly inward. Because they have seen the good qualities of meditation, they should subdue the mind in meditative tranquility. Because wise people have seen the negative qualities of distraction, they do not take enjoyment in it, and practice calm. They should calm envy, calm unhappiness.

"The person who observes spiritual precepts and who applies these techniques of thought will attain a mind that is naturally at rest. It will be habitual; no more effort is required. Then both body and mind will be totally trained. This is called 'engaging the mind.'"

For each of the nine meditative techniques explained above, you must abandon five faults. To do this, use the eight antidotes as they are needed.

You must come to recognize that among these five the two faults that are most important to overcome are laziness and agitation. If you experience laziness, reduce the portion of food you eat before you meditate, and sit on an elevated seat with a thin cushion. Recite petitionary and refuge prayers in a clear and full voice. Keep your body and your mind sharp and meditate.

If you become agitated, use the opposite methods to counter this. When you have calmed both laziness and agitation, meditate.

Water Similes for Meditation Experiences

Like Water Rushing Down a Steep Mountain: Once you are meditating in this way, an unending series of thoughts will arise from the depths, which you had not been able to discern with typical modes of attention. These thoughts have been in your mind all along, but you have never recognized them because you have never composed your mind in contemplation. "Now that you are aware of them, you may think, 'I have more thoughts than ever!' or, 'I am not meditating!' But this is the first experience of meditation. It is called 'like water rushing down a steep mountain.'" This is the experience of recognizing your thoughts.

Like Water in a Deep Narrow Canyon: Even while this is occurring, do not delay your meditation. Reduce the flow of thoughts as you can and continue meditating. Through this you will sense the flow of your thoughts coming to rest. But as soon as it comes to rest, the flow starts up again! Flowing and ceasing—in this way the stream of thoughts will alternate. This is the second experience of meditation. It is called "like water in a deep and narrow canyon." This is the experience of bringing your thoughts to rest.

Like a Pond at the Confluence of Three Valleys: Now, conscientiously meditating upon the flow of these thoughts, at some point they will collectively become nonconceptual, just like sneezes can stop all of a sudden. Set an intense awareness upon this experience and meditate further. At times you will simply be conscious of your surroundings, though thoughts will still

suddenly arise as well. This is the third experience of meditation. It is called "like a pond at the confluence of three valleys."
This is the experience of your thought becoming fatigued.

Like Ocean Waves: Meditate once again on the remaining
flow of thoughts, and most of the stream of thoughts will be
calmed. Your mind will become comfortably settled in a single point. In this state you may have one or two successive
thoughts, but they will come to rest as soon as they arise.
This is the fourth experience of meditation. It is called "like
ocean waves." This is the experience of waves of thought.

Like an Ocean without Waves: Meditate once again on
this flow of thoughts. All remaining thoughts will be calmed.
This is resting with a single-pointed mind. The mind's quality is clear. This is the fifth experience of meditation. It is
called "like an ocean without waves." It is the experience of
thoughts being calmed.

Cultivating Bright Clarity of Consciousness

Now your thoughts are settled and calmed, and your mind
rests stably and single-pointedly. However, you may not have
achieved a bright clarity of consciousness. This experience is
the calm resting of churning thoughts. You must meditate to
retain the single-pointed mind cultivating the bright clarity
of consciousness until it is like a flame that is not disturbed
by the wind. If this clarity of consciousness appears above
and beyond the objects of the senses, then, without focusing
on your meditation object, focus your attention right inside
your mind and stabilize the clarity of consciousness upon
that. If you get lazy or agitated, use the means described earlier to regain clarity. Then rest naturally, without making an
effort, in the state of bright clarity of consciousness.

Meditate in Good Health

When you have refined your practice in this way, continue
meditating. If your meditative state is lacking at the beginning of a meditation session and yet you eventually achieve a

good state by the end of a session, you need energy at the beginning, so meditate with greater energy. But if after doing this your mind wanders and does not want to remain settled, or if you become physically or mentally fatigued, this is the result of too much energy. If this happens, relax your meditation again.

Eat only as much food as you need to keep you in good health. Keep your health up by sleeping at night, not during the day. Meditate persistently only when you are in good health.

Contemplating the Significance of Meditation Practice

How should you contemplate the significance of such meditation? In a quiet place sit on a comfortable seat in the meditation posture of Vairocana. Recite the refuge prayer, the petitionary prayers to your mentors, the vow to become enlightened, and other preliminaries. Then say to yourself:

> "Oh, how my mind has been buffeted by the winds of cyclic existence from the very beginning! Whatever the mind wants to do it just does. My mind has been incapable of single-pointedly focusing on an object of virtue for so much as the time it takes to snap my fingers! So I have been unable to bring myself across the ocean of cyclic existence, and I have been unable to assist others to achieve their own liberation. How terrible!
>
> "Now I will rely on the advice of a spiritual mentor of integrity and gain the distinctive satisfaction that comes from totally purifying my body and my mind. I will settle my mind in single-pointed meditative equilibrium and attain complete enlightenment."

Investigating Your Emotions

Now, stop breathing erratically or in any exaggerated or noisy manner. Count twenty-one sets of inhalation and exhalation, making no mistake in the count. Through this bring your body and your mind into balance.

Investigate whether the thoughts in your mind are harsh. If you have obvious attachment to objects of desire, and the bulk of your thoughts are desirous, calm these thoughts with methods such as contemplating the impurities of the body or other objects. Do the same in the case of hatred by contemplating loving-kindness.

To counter ignorance, consider the interdependent arising of phenomena. Counter jealousy by putting yourself in the other's situation. Counter pride by putting them in your place, or by meditating on the dissolution of the component parts of the body.

Now, investigate once more whether there are impurities apparent in your mind or not. If there are, employ the methods to counteract whichever are present. You may no longer be under the sway of an impure mind or worldly modes of thought. However, when such patterns of thought do enter your mind, remember the point of the instructions given just above, and first concentrate your mind upon your object of meditation.

Be sure to settle your mind there with no laziness or agitation. If you concentrate too intensely and produce agitation, make sure to be mindful and alert in a relaxed manner during the concentration. If you become too relaxed and you are overcome with drowsiness, settle your mind on itself in such a way that you are comfortably aware of the clarity of the meditation without the mind feeling forced.

Refining the Corrective Measures in Meditation

So the first two of this three-part method are the application of correctives to both laziness and agitation. The third part is balancing out the corrective measures once laziness and agitation are calmed. In whatever kind of contemplative practice you do, these three corrective measures are very important.

By meditating in this way, all application of conceptual thought should be calmed. Rather, what remains beyond that for long periods of time should be the vivid, clear sense of consciousness.

Once you become stable in this, you should no longer look directly at the object of meditation. Instead, look more and more at the clearly appearing radiance of the mind itself. And once you experience this clarity vividly, relax your mind upon just that. Do not differentiate the past from the present. Do not look forward to the future. Do not list out your current affairs. Instead, whatever good or bad thoughts arise, just cut them off as soon as they arise. Settle yourself so that you are both outwardly observant and inwardly at ease.

After the Meditation Session

When you get up from your meditation session, make sure that you leave your contemplations in a positive manner. Dedicate any virtues you may have accumulated and freshen your senses. Even when you are in between meditation sessions, be sure not to lose that sense of quiet solitude. Give up all the causes of mental distraction and agitation.

Begin your next meditation session soon. When you first start, you should make the sessions short. After you have accustomed yourself to meditation, make the sessions longer. Eventually you will be able to conduct a session throughout an entire day and night. Until then, practice.

CHAPTER SIX

WIDER PERSPECTIVE

INTRODUCTION

"Recognize whatever thoughts arise, and do not apply any further elaboration on them. Settle yourself in an unwavering state and cultivate this practice."

This chapter presents the meditation practice that, along with calm meditation, is essential for many other types of meditation: insight meditation. Where calm meditation aims to still the mind so that, free of uncontrolled thoughts and emotions, it can focus, insight meditation uses the enhanced capacity for focus to investigate the workings of thought and emotion themselves.

Calm meditation and insight meditation are typically discussed as a pair within the same teaching. Here we pair calm and insight meditation in chapters 5 and 6, yet we switch traditions as we move from calm to insight. All the major schools of Tibetan Buddhism have characteristic teachings on the common techniques of meditation. We transition now from the Three Visions literature of the Sakya School to the Great Seal teachings of the Kagyu School. Where the Three Visions provided tools—breathing techniques, metaphors, corrective measures for reining in and refining our contemplative patters of thought and emotion—this chapter takes us into the labyrinth of thought and emotion and prompts us to use the assured and tranquil capacity for focus to follow the threads that lead through the labyrinth.

The text translated in this chapter is *The Great Seal Dispel-*

ling the Darkness of Ignorance. As the title says, this is a meditation instruction from the Great Seal tradition, an Indian style of contemplative thought and practice that became popular with the Kagyu School in Tibet, so popular that Tibetan writers advanced the theory and practice of Great Seal meditation beyond what is found in Indian texts. The author of *Dispelling the Darkness of Ignorance* was one of the great writers on meditation of the Karma branch of the Kagyu School, the Ninth Karmapa Wangchuk Dorjé (1556–1603). The "darkness of ignorance" refers in a general sense to a lack of experience-based understanding of the mind. More specifically, "ignorance" here is unawareness of the impermanent nature of reality, which, when coupled with basic unhealthy emotions and behaviors such as greed and hatred, is a root cause of human suffering. Meditation is, in this text, and in the Great Seal tradition more broadly, a key tool for overcoming ignorance, and therefore for reducing—and in the most utopian sense totally eradicating—suffering.

The Ninth Karmapa's *Dispelling the Darkness of Ignorance* is refreshing for its relatively informal style; it does not quote classic Indian Buddhist scripture, and it is not overly systematic. Rather, it emulates the voice of a meditation teacher walking a student through the steps of encountering, observing, and analyzing one's thoughts and emotions in real time as they arise and cease. There are eight sections in the passage translated here, each presenting a distinct practice within insight meditation. The first four are called pointing-out instructions. Each of these introduces the practitioner to a particular aspect of the workings of thought and emotion, and provides scripts, or perhaps thought experiments, that the practitioner can use to begin to "look attentively" at this particular feature of mind.

Every section opens with a call to begin a formal meditation session, taking up the posture (as described in chapter 2) and calming one's thoughts and emotions (chapter 5). With this as a basis, the specific meditation begins. The first of the pointing-out instructions is called "Inspecting the Essence of

Mind." The beginning of the investigation of "the funda-mental condition of your mind" proceeds with a series of questions: "Does your mind's fundamental condition have color, form, or shape? Does it arise, remain, and recede? Or not?" Questions such as these are essential to the four pointing-out instructions. They orient meditators toward their thoughts and emotions, but they also orient them to potentially larger capacities and states. For the Kagyu tradition and related forms of Buddhism argue that there is awareness that (at least at the outset of practice) stands apart from the quick, darting movements of thought and emotion. It stands still. And even though it is still, it is not inert. It is energetic, vibrant, thriving. A common way to try to capture this vivid, basic awareness in language is to use metaphors of light. The fundamental nature of the mind is clear awareness; it is "lucid," it is "sparkling." But the meditation does not emphasize this point at first.

Rather, in the first pointing-out instruction, the practitio-ner is urged to start noticing the sheer variety of the mind and its mental workings. So much is going on! Thoughts come; thoughts go. Emotions chase after thoughts, and thoughts give rise to emotions. There are multiple viewpoints available at any given moment; the thoughts and feelings themselves, the sense of vibrant bare awareness, light and vibrant yet distinct from a given thought, a given object of thought, a given emo-tion. And then there is the perspective of "the meditator," a third perspective that can look at what else is going on in the mind. This perspective can investigate the thoughts and emo-tions even as it can the sense of an illuminating energy. This is an awareness that somehow stands apart from both the thought and the thinker.

Questions are, again, a key tool in these exercises. *Dispel-ling the Darkness of Ignorance* is not overly didactic here, though it certainly has a point of view. Statements about the nature of the mind and reality come more quickly in the second set of four insight meditation practices, the recogni-tion instructions. Here, in the pointing-out instructions, question after question urges the meditator to open the mind to multiple forms of inquiry, to keep an "open mind," if you will, about the mind as one familiarizes oneself with the inner landscape.

Section two, "The Movement of Conceptual Thought," presents a classic contemplative inquiry into the workings of thought, dedicated to the triad of "coming, staying, and going." Where does a thought come from? Where is it when it is "with you," an object within your conscious awareness? Where does it go when it passes from conscious awareness? There are not simple answers; that is not the point of this exercise. Exploration is key here, the act of attentive questioning, of turning the mind itself into a question to be pondered with focus, care, and patience. At the close of this section, the Ninth Karmapa emphasizes that the success of such inquiry should be decided in conversation with one's teacher: "The meditation teacher and disciple will decide together, based on discussion and impressions, whether the student's attentive looking has gone well, and if there has been progress in determining the nature of thought." The same goes for the other seven techniques in this chapter.

Section three takes up another foundational premise in Buddhist meditation, that "appearances and mind are inseparable." The basic idea is that our conceptual capacity so strongly determines our perception that it is more accurate to say that thought constitutes objects rather than objects exist separately from either thought or perception. The coiled rope that is mistaken for a snake is a classic example in Buddhist philosophy; we "see" a snake because we interpret an object based on a conceptual image (which is fueled by emotional energy, in this case fear), and thus we attribute a sense of reality to an object, the snake, that is just not there. Buddhism claims that this example illustrates how our daily perception works in general. We attribute features that are purely conceptual or emotional to neutral objects, and thus create objects of perception that are already concepts, already part and parcel of our thoughts, our minds. In this way, "appearances," objects that we see, feel, taste, or experience through the senses, are inseparable from our thoughts and emotions, from our minds.

There is a long tradition of philosophical literature on this topic in Buddhism, but that is not the tactic that *Dispelling the Darkness of Ignorance* takes. Rather, the Ninth Karmapa asks meditators to ask themselves how objects of perception, "appearances," come to seem the way that they do, and to ask themselves what role the mind plays in the formation of those appearances. Buddhist philosophy has answers for those questions, but here the emphasis is on showing and experiencing rather than telling and arguing. Throughout this section, the questions ask the practitioner to move deftly from perspective to perspective, shifting focus from the object to the thought, to the consciousness—that of the meditator—and back again. In this way, the exercise trains the meditator in the fine arts of introspection, cultivating the skills to both recognize and utilize the multiple features of thought.

The final pointing-out instruction moves from appearance and mind to take on another seeming dichotomy, that between the stillness and movement of the mind. Is there a part of the mind that is "still," that somehow remains in a fixed place or state as it perceives the "movement" of other thoughts or emotions? If so, where does it stay, and where do the moving pieces move? This contemplative exercise moves meditators further into the space that, seemingly, contains the many aspects of consciousness, and asks them to consider whether spatial metaphors are even the right way to understand the workings of the mind and emotion.

At the heart of these exercises lies the core Buddhist idea that the mind is, before it is divided and subdivided into subject, object, and emotional reaction, a kind of basic awareness that is both tranquil and clear. Awareness, on this view, is "luminous." Here, too, there is a long philosophical tradition, as well as great debate, on the nature of this luminous awareness. But this text is not about philosophical argument; it is about cultivating a certain experience. At the close of section four, the Ninth Karmapa says that this "clear aspect of the mind should be present even as the grasping aspect of the mind is absent, like a child looking around a temple." What a beautiful image, and what a beautiful simile for the type of inquisitive openness that the pointing-out instructions seek to cultivate in practitioners.

The second set of sections is called "Four Introductions to Recognizing the Mind." These cover much of the same ground as the first four sections, though, this time, the pointing-out instructions emphasize enhancing and maintaining the insights gained in the first four practices. Where the contemplative practitioner first had to have a given feature of thought and emotion "pointed out" to them, here the meditator who has some experience of looking at the mind may now be prepared to "recognize" the phenomenon when they encounter it again. And if they are not ready in the estimation of their contemplative mentor, the recognition instructions offer more robust statements on the nature of the mind, as opposed to the primarily interrogative technique of the pointing-out instructions. In this way meditators move from early exploratory ventures along the pathways of the mind to more purposeful periods of focused attention on the places they have already visited, aided by statements that tell the practitioner what they will encounter when investigating the mind.

The first of the four "introductions to recognizing the mind" looks again at the fundamental nature of the mind, the topic of the first pointing-out instruction. Unlike the pointing-out instruction, this teaching is more direct in giving an answer to the question, What is the fundamental nature of the mind? "The nature of the resting mind is clear, vivid, and bare, though not simply nothingness. It is an awareness that is without a reference point. It is lucid, bright, a relaxed clarity." This section introduces other key terms for the clear, luminous nature of the mind, or bare awareness, for example. "Ordinary mind" is important for its affirmation that this lucid clarity is the more basic state of consciousness, as opposed to conceptual thought that involves the separation of a subject doing the perceiving and the object being perceived.

The second section (number six from the overall sequence of eight sections) emphasizes the difficulty in trying to talk about the workings of the mind. This is because language distinguishes between a subject and an object as a matter of course. And if appearances and mind are in fact one, or if the fundamental nature of the mind is lucid clarity without differentiation into separable components, then to talk of subject and object is inaccurate. Because talk necessarily creates a subject and object, any use of language already misses the point of the fundamentally unified and clear awareness that is consciousness. Therefore, this contemplative tradition of Buddhism typically does not trust language to serve as anything more than a rough sketch of reality. (It is this distrust of straightforward language that leads some contemplative writers to use poetry and its metaphorical power to evoke a sense of the mind's natural awareness, as we see throughout this book's chapters.) It is the experience of that reality that counts. Keeping this in mind, the exercises in this passage encourage the meditator to experience the ways in which the clear, lucid mind, "ordinary mind," is in fact the same awareness as conceptual thought that distinguishes subject and object. There is unity in the mind where once we saw only dichotomy.

Sections three and four return to earlier topics as well: three to the unity of objects of appearance and the thoughts that grasp those objects, and four to the unity of the purported stillness of lucid, clear mind, and the seeming movement of conceptual thought and its objects. In contrast to the first introductions to these topics, these passages come right out and state that there is no difference between appearance and thought, between the stillness and movement of thought. All this experience is unified, as is the more fundamental capacity of awareness itself.

And this is good news, according to Buddhist contemplative tradition, for this awareness is nothing more or less than the potential to see, to feel, and finally to live beyond the negative modes of thought and behavior that lead us to suffer, and to cause others to suffer. Beginning to recognize this awareness, for the Kagyu School as well as other schools of

Tibetan Buddhism, is a key for cultivating oneself as a more compassionate human being. The insight meditation chapter ends here, on a high note: "When you have joined calm meditation with insight meditation, contemplative experiences and realization will begin to develop. This constitutes the beginning of the path to enlightenment."

Dispelling the Darkness of Ignorance can be deceptively simple at times; its instructions are straightforwardly given, yet beyond the sitting and breathing techniques discussed in earlier chapters, the action of insight meditation one is instructed to undertake is, quite literally, all in one's mind. Buddhist contemplative tradition knows that teaching introspection is profoundly challenging, because one person cannot be in the thoughts of another, and thus cannot precisely know the movements, the ebb and flow, of that vast, uncharted sea that is another human being's mind. How then does anyone teach another the skills to investigate their own mind so thoroughly that they can actually improve their mind, their thoughts, their emotions? This challenge is one reason why Tibetan tradition recommends that meditation practice be learned with the guidance of experienced, authoritative teachers. Much like the best coaches mentor their athletes based upon understanding of the sport acquired through their own experience, so meditation teachers have, ideally, deep experience in the practice themselves.

The Ninth Karmapa models this coach-athlete relationship to great effect in *Dispelling the Darkness of Ignorance*. He uses language that is confident as well as informal to guide the practitioner through these meditation sessions, giving basic instructions on the steps to take and the moves to make, pointing out potential pitfalls, or pausing the practitioner so that they step back from a given practice to reflect on the meaning and context of practice in general. Each of the eight topics is in fact composed of a series of smaller, mini exercises. These are designated by the dividing markers (❈ ❈ ❈) in the translation. It may be useful to read this insight meditation chapter from *Dispelling the Darkness of Ignorance* once or twice all the way through, and then to read section by section, exercise by exercise. Each one benefits from savoring, from sitting with it to see where it takes you.

DISPELLING THE DARKNESS OF IGNORANCE, BY THE NINTH KARMAPA

Here are four ways of looking at mind:

One. Inspecting the Essence of Mind

The topic is insight meditation. Take up your posture as usual. Your gaze is very important here; your eyes should not blink, wander, or lose focus. Rather, you should look straight ahead at the empty space directly in front of you.

In state of flawless stability, set your mind in a naturally tranquil state. Your mind should not try to make up anything about itself, nor focus on the self, nor be too alert.

Now energize your mind slightly and develop a moment of undistracted mindfulness that is lucid and wide awake.

Look attentively at the fundamental condition of your mind during this time of positive, robust calm meditation:

Does your mind's fundamental condition have color, form, or shape?

Does it arise, remain, and recede? Or not?

Is it inside, outside, or located somewhere else?

Aside from your mind, is there something else there to be discerned?

Is your mind an empty nothingness that cannot be identified?

Or is there something in that calm state that is a lucid, pure, and clear awareness that transcends identification and is inexpressible?

Is the fundamental condition of this settled mind a totally oblivious form of knowing, or is it a sparkling, wide-awake, fresh form of knowing?

❊ ❊ ❊ ❊ ❊

The fundamental nature of reality is the overarching key point here. Therefore, if your thoughts are compelled by the eight worldly phenomena (gain and loss, fame and infamy, praise and blame, and pleasure and sorrow), and because of these you use intellectualism or high-sounding lingo to say, "My meditative realization is so, so good," you have not actually developed this fundamental nature of reality. You are just spinning your own head around! You are deceiving yourself.

What's more, if you have taken spiritual vows, you have broken your vow by using worldly dharma to imitate the experiences of a spiritual master. So practice your meditation with great perseverance. Do not patch up your external experience with concepts. Rather, internally, you must develop a genuine experience of realization through the power of your meditative practice.

❊ ❊ ❊ ❊ ❊

Now, tighten up your awareness and look at your mind. Then relax and look again. You must look at the fundamental condition of the mind at rest. During this process, place your mind in a state of lucid, shining clarity, like the sun in a cloudless sky.

❊ ❊ ❊ ❊ ❊

The first pointing-out instruction is making an effort to look at the fundamental condition of the mind with alert awareness. Therefore, teachers must question and train their students according to their estimation of the student's mental range. Sometimes a student will deceive the teacher into thinking they are suitable for meditation training. So questioning the student is extremely important to determine whether they have had a meditation experience, or a realization, some ordinary experience, or are just talking in dharma lingo. Teachers must point their observations out to the student. And students must also make such an effort.

This is the first pointing-out instruction on the fundamental condition of the mind.

Two. The Movement of Conceptual Thought

You have investigated the foundation of the mind, and now you must be introduced to investigating the wanderings of conceptual thought, how it moves in the present movement.

Set your posture and gaze, as well as your behavior, as we have discussed previously. Your mind should be relaxed and lucid, in a state that is harmonious, clear, and nonconceptual.

While in this state, give rise to a fleeting thought, or produce some suitable thought, and look at the nature of that emergent thought.

Look at the time it takes to emerge. Look at the location of its emergence.

Does it have color, or shape?

Where does it emerge?

Where does it stay?

Where does it recede?

Is it outside or inside the body?

If it is inside, where is it?

In the center of your heart?

Investigate where thought is: inside, outside, or where?

❁ ❁ ❁ ❁ ❁

Investigate how thought arises.

Is this mind a thing, or is it a non-thing?

Does it arise and recede?

Does it have color or shape?

If it does arise and recede, or have color and shape, what are these like?

If you think, "It does not," then what about the speech that says that. Is that something?

If you think, "This is it," then even though there may be no movement of thought, there is something knowable such as neither arising nor receding.

When you look at a thought, is it the case that all thought is empty, free from elaboration, and without arising and receding? Or perhaps when you have looked at that thought, it then slips away without any trace?

Look carefully! Do thoughts arise even if their origins and measure cannot be identified?

And if they do arise yet cannot be identified, when a thought does arise and you think, "That is the part that cannot be identified," well, is that an identifiable thought or not?

❀ ❀ ❀ ❀ ❀

When a thought arises, or when you have produced a thought, look at its nature without shutting it down or grasping onto it. If it was a pleasurable or an unpleasurable thought, look at the nature of that pleasurableness or unpleasurableness.

However many thoughts you have, keep looking at them. Even if intense thoughts and emerging negative emotions such as the five poisons arise, even if you produce them, keep looking.

Ask, "Is there any distinctive mental event in the thought itself, or the object of that thought, or the thoughts preceding them?"

Look without affirming or denying anything about these thoughts. Look to gain decisive certainty.

❀ ❀ ❀ ❀ ❀

If you see the nature of thought with clear awareness, is that clear awareness that rests prior to thought and that clear awareness that sees the current thought the same or different?

If you cannot determine this, then send the thought back and settle your mind into clear awareness. When you are not thinking and a thought suddenly pops up, look at the nature of that clear awareness, which is unaffected by any normal thought that may have previously occurred.

❀ ❀ ❀ ❀ ❀

In short, the meditation teacher and disciple will decide together, based on discussion and impressions, whether the student's attentive looking has gone well, and if there has been progress in determining the nature of thought.

Persevere in this method of looking at thoughts, which is the second pointing-out instruction.

Three. Recognizing That Appearances and Mind Are Inseparable

Now you will be introduced to the inseparability of the mind and appearing phenomena by looking from the perspective of appearances.

Set your gaze and posture as before. Now set your eyes and your attention upon a distinct object such as a pillar, a pot, a statue, (imagined image such as) Mount Meru, or another appropriate image in front of you. Relax your awareness of it, then look again.

In a similar manner, attend to the fundamental state of sound that is an object for your ears, noting if there is a difference between pleasant or unpleasant sounds, or loud or soft, or between your voice and another's.

Now attend to a smell that appears as an object to your nose, noting if it is good or bad.

Now a taste on the tongue; is it tasty or not?

Now a feeling upon your body: Is it pleasant, unpleasant, hot, or cold? Troubling? Painful?

❋ ❋ ❋ ❋ ❋

Look attentively at whatever may arise. While you are looking, does the phenomenon cease or does it remain? Do you and the phenomenon appear separately? Or do your mind and the phenomena arise together? Or does your mind say, "I, the mind, am appearing, so this is appearing," and then externalizes this appearance?

The appearing phenomenon and the mind are inseparable. Therefore, the phenomenon is a non-object vividly arising as an empty appearance.

❋ ❋ ❋ ❋ ❋

Expand your attentive looking to the conceptual thought that is doing the looking and the act of attending to the five sense objects. Look to see if they really are two things. Look to see if there is any difference at all between the appearing object and the conceptual thought that grasps the object.

When you look at an object and that object is vividly over there, is it really as you think it is? If you do not think that it is, then it would seem that there is no difference at all between that object that is unobstructed and unobscured and the mind looking that is relaxed, that doesn't grasp, and that does not separate subject from object.

❀ ❀ ❀ ❀ ❀

Now, if there is no reason to imagine that the object is not really as you think it is, and if that object really is over there, then how about the thought itself that thinks, "It's really over there"? Where is that? Pay attention to this.

❀ ❀ ❀ ❀ ❀

In a similar manner, look at whether your mind and your body are the same thing or distinct things.

If they are the same thing, then are your body, which develops and decays, and your mind, which does not develop and decay, a single permanent entity, or distinct permanent entities?

If they are distinct, then the body and the mind must be recognizable as separate things.

However, the mind is not located in one place; it pervades the body. It doesn't exist just at the top of your body, or at the bottom. How is it that you can experience feelings?

Your body and your mind are the support and the supported. Yet if the body is the exterior and the mind is the interior, just like a person in their clothing, then you might think that the body alone should be able to experience feeling. And if you think that, then even a corpse would necessarily experience feeling.

If you think that the mind is what experiences feeling, then the two, body and mind, are separate. But the mind cannot be killed or divided at all.

So if it is your mind that feels it when your body is pricked by a thorn, would it not be the same as when the clothes (the support) are burned, the person (the supported) is also burned? You must investigate this thoroughly and resolve this for yourself.

❁ ❁ ❁ ❁ ❁

Throughout this work, understand that every feeling that arises is a wave and your mind is like water. Settle yourself in this awareness, and from this state you can cut through to your mind's natural state.

This is the third form of attentive looking.

Four. Establishing How the Mind Both Stays Still and Moves

Now look attentively once again at the fundamental state of your mind when it is resting lucidly in luminous emptiness. And once again produce a conceptual thought and look at its fundamental state.

Are the fundamental states of these two, the resting mind and the moving mind, the same or different?

If you look in this way and you see them to be different, how are they different? Do these two, resting and moving, arise one upon the other, like two threads stretched out and then wound tightly together?

Or is the resting mind like the field, and the moving mind like the crops that grow upon it? Is that how they arise?

Or are they coiled, like a snake or a rope, such that the two are as one? If so, when either one is resting without proceeding forth, it is not moving, and when either one is moving, it is not resting.

You might say, "Yet the moving mind proliferates many random thoughts quickly. And the resting mind is settled and immobile. So there is a huge difference between the two! So they have distinct fundamental natures." Well, if you think this, then is the difference a matter of color, or shape, or something else? Or is the difference in their rising, remaining, receding, or past, present, and future? Or perhaps the difference is one of permanence versus impermanence? Look attentively at this.

❉ ❉ ❉ ❉ ❉

As you become aware of your conceptual thoughts during meditation, you will see that resting and moving thought have the same fundamental nature. They appear one upon the other. When the mind is resting, there is no thinker that moves, and when the mind is moving, there is no thinker that rests.

Like water and waves, these are the activities of a singular mind. There is only this. Rest and movement are nothing more than bare, luminous emptiness. If you realize this, then you have achieved a modest realization.

❉ ❉ ❉ ❉ ❉

And yet, when you bring forward a conceptual thought and settle it in meditation, is it within luminous emptiness? Or does the thought disappear, and after that there is luminous emptiness? Or perhaps the thought itself is clear and that is what becomes luminous emptiness?

If you think it may be one of the first two, then make some strong prayers to your teacher and make an effort to look again so that you can be certain how you see it!

❉ ❉ ❉ ❉ ❉

Some people engaged in such attentive looking at the fundamental nature of the mind are of the type who can make a leap, cultivating insight first and then calm meditation, or perhaps cultivating both at the same time. Owing to their prior training, those who cultivate the two simultaneously develop both insight meditation and calm meditation just through being taught the texts. Those who cultivate them gradually do so in stages. Here we are teaching in terms of the second of these types.

Look attentively according to the instructions for developing insight and calm. The clear aspect of the mind should be present even as the grasping aspect of the mind is absent, like a child looking around a temple. Settle yourself, and while you are in this state, work hard to look attentively. Make an effort. Do not be lazy. Renounce everything you don't need with conviction and enter a state of firm and unfabricated mindfulness that is faithful, dedicated, and unwavering.

Do not be bound by your hopes and fears. Do not veer into a sloppy sort of contemplative practice. Work only toward a good next life. If you make this kind of effort to look attentively at your mind, there is no doubt that the wisdom that comes from insight meditation will develop.

This clarification of the resting mind and the moving mind is the fourth form of attentive looking.

FOUR INTRODUCTIONS TO RECOGNIZING THE MIND

One. The First Introduction

If you can look at the fundamental nature of the mind in this way, and you have cultivated the experiential instructions on the mind, then you may not need pointing-out instructions, for the mind will come to reveal itself.

However, there are people who do not recognize the mind even if all this has occurred. There are some who have only a dry intellectual grasp based on simply hearing about it, and hope that this will be sufficient to develop valuable contemplative experience.

The spiritual teacher must be able to distinguish these types of students. The student must reach the essential points of these teachings and integrate them into their contemplative experience. To this end, the first pointing-out instruction, geared toward those who are first looking at the fundamental nature of the mind, is as follows.

❋ ❋ ❋ ❋ ❋

Look attentively at the fundamental nature of the mind at rest, as was discussed previously. The nature of the resting mind is clear, vivid, and bare, though not simply nothingness. It is an awareness that is without a reference point. It is lucid, bright, a relaxed clarity.

Yet there is no reason to say that it has color or shape, or to describe it as being like this or that. The nature of the settled mind is awareness that is without a reference point as well as without obstructions. Clear. Pure. Bare. Bright and vivid.

This is not the type of thing for which you can think, "I didn't see it, now I do," or, "I didn't experience it, now I do," or, "I wasn't aware of this, and now I am." It cannot even be verbally expressed as something arising within you. You must determine this at a deep level. If you intellectualize it as something that is a clear and calm nothingness, this is not reliable, and little will come of it.

If your understanding of the nature of the mind comes from deep within, however, well, this is the arising of meditative insight in the resting mind. If you do not persevere in nakedly seeing the nature of the mind, the pointing-out instructions will result only in an intellectualized object, and in insensitivity to the nature of the mind. If this happens, other means of teaching you may actually cause harm. So the spiritual teacher should not put the pointing-out instructions to you until you have cut the stream of conceptual thought, for you will not see the fundamental nature of the mind. And if you have not glimpsed this nature, the pointing-out instructions are presently appropriate. If you are not introduced to the nature of the mind, you will not progress along the higher Path of Meditation.

❉ ❉ ❉ ❉ ❉

Now, when you have positive contemplative experiences, look attentively at them. When you have negative experiences, try again and again to recall the pointing-out instructions. Teachings on the means for achieving positive contemplative experience are called guidance instructions. When you know how to meditate, these guidance instructions are said to be complete. So, in that context, cultivate your meditation steadily. As you develop contemplative experience and realization, you will see the fundamental nature of the mind without difficulty.

❋ ❋ ❋ ❋ ❋

So, in order to achieve definite awareness and resolve any doubts, the spiritual teacher should point out the following to you:

Meditation consists generally of both calm and insight. Calm is when your mind settles down into its natural state, all conceptual thought calms down just where it is, and the mind rests, clear and serene.

In this state regular thinking does not engage with the distractions of this life. Rather, your mind is peaceful, at ease, with all negative motions calm, as in an easy sleep. Your mind rests with singular attention on the fundamental nature of virtue, and you are able to remain in this state as long as you like. You do not even notice that you are breathing in and out.

Is your meditation like this? If so, this is excellent calm meditation. The contemplative experiences here are crucial. You should not take them to be realizations of enlightenment, but still, you need them. Cultivate such experience without being attached to it. Do not let yourself slide from a meditative calm into drowsiness or overexcitement or apathy.

The fundamental nature of the mind is beyond verbalization or even conceptualization, so you can't say, "It is like this," or say it has color or shape. You cannot say, "It's like this," or, "It is experienced like this," in the way you can with an object or regular thought. It is more like the sensual pleasure of an inexperienced person. It is the integration of clarity and emptiness, and it is free of all limits imposed by trying to identify it or elaborate on it.

It is not subject to any conceptual thought that treats phenomena. It is not troubled by worldly conceptual thought. It is not measured by vagaries such as "calm meditation" or "conceptuality." Such awareness is settled in its own state, existing just where it is.

It is the root of all good qualities. It is called "ordinary awareness" or just "mind."

If you are not aware of this "ordinary awareness," you will be existentially ignorant and keep spinning within this cyclic existence. If you are aware, you will have wisdom, or specifically the "wisdom that simultaneously arises with enlightenment." This is called "the natural" or "clear light" or "insight meditation." So you must distinguish the signs of cyclic existence from those of liberation.

❋ ❋ ❋ ❋ ❋

The spiritual teacher introduces you to the fundamental nature of the mind, and you will recognize it like someone you have met before. That recognition is called "recognizing the mind." This is not produced by a smart student who just studies the spiritual teacher's instructions. Your negative emotions and conceptual thoughts obscure this ordinary mind, which has existed in this way forever, and you do not recognize it. But now the continuous flow of conceptual thought has been interrupted, you have been introduced to it, and you are aware of it.

The mind is a lucid clarity that cannot be objectively identified. Not having any inherent nature itself, it is sheer vividness. Its fundamental nature is uninterrupted intense vividness. This is the nature of the mind. Cultivate a steady bare recognition of this nature, and it will be of inestimable benefit to you.

❋ ❋ ❋ ❋ ❋

This dawning of insight is an introduction, so it is the first actual pointing-out instruction. Delve deep into its essential meaning. It is immensely important that you integrate this into your contemplative experience and cultivate it at all times. So recognize the nature of the mind and cultivate it.

Two. The Second Way of Looking

The second method of attentively looking determines the nature of thought. There are two pointing-out instructions. The first is pointing out in reference to the nonconceptual mind. The second is pointing out in reference to presently occurring conceptual thought, which can be either when a thought arises or when you cause one to arise.

❋ ❋ ❋ ❋ ❋

The first is as follows: You have looked at the clear and vivid resting mind, an awareness that is not affected by either drowsiness or overexcitement. You know that you cannot say it has color or shape. You know that there is no reason to think, "It has no arising and no receding," and yet you are aware that it has no arising and receding. This is the dawn of insight meditation on nonconceptual thought.

❋ ❋ ❋ ❋ ❋

The second is as follows: If you simply assert, "All moving conceptual thought is free of arising and receding," you are just empty talk. If you relaxedly recognize with no lasting impression, without identifying arising, receding, abiding, color, shape, and so forth, this is a modest dawning of insight.

You should not even have the thought "I am not explicitly identifying these." Rather, thoughts should arise and recede simultaneously without your explicitly identifying them, without seizing on their lack of importance. When this occurs, this is the pointing-out instruction.

❋ ❋ ❋ ❋ ❋

Additionally, understand that there is no difference between conceptual thought and the object of conceptual thought, between the mind at rest or moving, between a past state of mind and a past conceptual thought. All of this is clear, bare awareness.

When you bring up a conceptual thought and it fades, that thought has not receded into clear emptiness; the very thought that pops up arises as clear emptiness. If you understand this, this is the recognition introduction.

Moving conceptual thought, the resting mind, and the fundamental nature of thought are all bare, clear emptiness. What's more, the understanding of this, as well as of nonconceptuality, is exactly the same as the consciousness that does not recognize this, overestimates them, and holds on to either one.

Earlier you did not recognize conceptual thoughts, so they could not be a part of your meditation. They constituted unawareness. Now that you recognize them, you can meditate on them directly. They now constitute awareness. They have become wisdom.

Now make the basis of your meditation conceptual thoughts. Prior to this, conceptual thoughts obscured themselves and you could not see them.

This meditation on conceptual thoughts is better than meditation on non-conceptuality. You now know how to meditate on conceptual thought. So take whatever thoughts do arise as just what you should recognize for what it is.

If no thoughts arise, rest in that state of non-arising; there is no need to cultivate more thoughts. If they do arise, remain in this state; there is no need to rein them in. Do not give any thought to your expectations or apprehensions; make the fundamental nature of meditation conceptual thought itself.

For conceptual thought is no more than mind, and this mind is by nature self-liberating, bare, clear emptiness. It is the enlightened body of reality, and as such transcends the distinction between that which liberates and that which must be liberated. So understanding in this way is the beginning of insight meditation on conceptual thought. This is the recognition introduction to the unity of clarity and emptiness, which is the enlightened body of reality.

In briefest terms: Recognize whatever thoughts arise, and do not apply any further elaboration on them. Settle yourself in an unwavering state and cultivate this practice.

This is the second actual recognition introduction. And yet, recognition alone is not enough; you need to cultivate this as a continuous state.

Three. The Inseparability of Appearances and Mind

The third type of recognition introduction is about appearances, or rather the inseparability of appearances and mind.

Look attentively at any of the five sense objects (a sight, touch, smell, sound, or taste); there is an unobstructed object, but you can't think, "That object is over there." And there is the mind, which looks at that object. But it does not grasp that object. In fact, these two, mind and object, are not in any way distinct. What's more, you cannot even think, "They are not different."

Body and mind are one. They are inseparable, not the least bit distinct. And clear emptiness and empty appearance are unified like the moon on water. Feelings of hot, cold, and so forth are likewise appearances. You do not recognize such feelings to be empty appearances, so your mind reifies them and endlessly seizes onto them. Yet, beyond that, understand that in truth whatever your mind and body feel is in no way a base upon which you can conceptually posit something that is not there.

❀ ❀ ❀ ❀ ❀

Whatever appearances arise, fix your gaze and set your mind upon them.

Then relax your attention a bit and remain in that state; initially the object's fine distinctions stay on track. But then looking becomes unpleasant, you become nauseated, or your eyes become sore or watery, which makes the object dissipate naturally. If then you look a bit more, a vivid appearance that is ungraspable emerges and again dissipates naturally.

During all this, your mind and the appearances are inseparable. They are empty appearances vividly arising as non-objects. And this is the self-appearance of reality itself. This is the defining characteristic of the mind; external appearances and the internal mind are not two distinct things. There is just the uninhibited arising of the natural expression of mind.

And yet we seize onto appearances as if they were objects. The act of "knowing" is just this seizing, which gives rise to mistaken understanding. And while mind and appearances cannot be isolated from each other, at this moment the mind misunderstands itself, and appears to itself.

Therefore, beyond mind-appearances there is no appearance that can be proven to be an object apart from mind. Yet due to our previous lack of awareness, or in other words the obscuration brought on by mental seizing upon an object, we do not see this.

❈ ❈ ❈ ❈ ❈

Now you can disrupt the flow of grasping conceptual thought and recognize appearances as non-objects. When you do not seize upon appearances, they become clear emptiness. They vividly appear as non-objects. Here appearances and emptiness arise simultaneously. This is referred to as light rays of the enlightened body of reality.

Cultivate this experience now, without any pretense. Give way to your senses and cultivate your contemplative practice directly upon appearances.

While in this state, let your awareness be relaxed and at ease and, without artifice, place your awareness upon the way that appearances actually are. Do not try to make your pleasure more pleasurable, your clarity clearer, your emptiness more empty, or your good works better. Do not hope for the future. Do not think of the past. Do not consider the present. Do not meditate with your intellect. Do not analyze the experience into "is" or "is not."

Your mind is itself natural, effortless, fresh. So do not struggle to guard it. Settle your mind into a state of the mind's own fundamental nature. Appearances and emptiness are inseparable. Sound and emptiness are inseparable. Pleasure and emptiness—inseparable. Awareness and emptiness—inseparable. Clarity and emptiness—inseparable. Settle yourself within this inseparability.

Appearances and emptiness are inseparable, so understand appearances clearly, without either inhibiting or seizing upon appearances.

When you do so, this is the development of insight meditation upon appearances. This is the recognition of the union of appearances and emptiness as being the enlightened body of reality.

Cultivate this meditation continuously and you will achieve stable contemplative experience and perfect realization.

Recognizing the fundamental nature of the mind directly in appearances is the third recognition introduction. This is the seventh contemplative practice you should cultivate.

Four. An Introduction to Recognizing Whether Staying Still and Moving Are the Same or Different

Now that you have looked attentively at whether the resting mind and the moving mind are the same or different, there is the following recognition introduction.

When you analyzed whether the resting mind and the moving mind are the same or different, you became aware of conceptual thought within the context of meditation. The resting mind and the moving mind are not distinct, though they arise in an alternating manner. When the mind is resting, it is not moving, and when it is moving, it is not at rest.

The active force here is nothing but the mind itself. The fundamental nature of both the mind at rest and the moving mind is bare clarity and emptiness, nothing else.

✻ ✻ ✻ ✻ ✻

Now, it is not the case that you provoke a conceptual thought and only then see bare clarity and emptiness. It is also not the case that the thought process dissipates and then proceeds into clear emptiness. That very thought that arises, at the moment it begins, is itself bare clarity and emptiness. When you understand this, you know the basic state of the mind.

You might say that the resting mind and the moving mind are fingers stretching from one hand; when the mind is not producing thoughts, it remains a vivid clarity, and when it is producing thoughts and moving, then the fundamental nature of these thoughts is bare clarity and emptiness, nothing else.

Now, all appearing objects are like waves upon water; there is in reality nothing that can be established beyond the illusory displays of the mind. When you realize this, this is recognition that appearances are of the mind.

❀ ❀ ❀ ❀ ❀

You have analyzed the mind in terms of arising, remaining, and receding, and found there is nothing that can be established. Like an elephant in a dream, there is in reality nothing that can be established. When you realize this, this is the recognition that the mind is empty.

Objects arise spontaneously and uninterruptedly from a state of empty, vivid clarity. When you realize this, this is the recognition that emptiness is spontaneous.

There is simply this spontaneity, an empty yet clear awareness spontaneously arisen, with no conceptual elaboration. Unchanging, it does not waver from a state of great harmony. This is just like a snake curling and uncurling; it arises and releases at the same time. When you are certain of this, this is the recognition that this spontaneity liberates itself.

The mind that you are coming to recognize is "ordinary mind," that very flickering awareness thinking one thing after another is itself the unity of clarity and emptiness. It is "great harmony." It possesses every perfect feature. This is called emptiness, or the Great Seal. When you recognize its nature, this is referred to as the realization of the Great Seal.

Therefore, without wavering even for a second, settle this vivid awareness just where it is, without meditating on anything. Relax without hope for a positive result or worrying about a negative result. Cultivate the "ordinary mind" in its own right. In that very instant, see the Great Seal, the unity of harmony and emptiness, like the sun in a pristine, cloudless sky.

When you have joined calm meditation with insight meditation, contemplative experiences and realization will begin to develop. This constitutes the beginning of the path to enlightenment.

❀ ❀ ❀ ❀ ❀

Emptiness is the essence of the mind. Clarity is the mind's defining characteristic, and the unity of these two is the fundamental nature of the mind. Is it good or bad? Does it arise, remain, and recede? Does it exist or not? Is it impermanent or not?

The fundamental nature of the mind is free from every limitation imposed by these questions! It transcends speech and ordinary thought. Its character cannot be seized upon. Yet it can be experienced in contemplation.

It goes by many names: bare, vivid clarity; the essence of harmony, clarity, and non-conceptuality; the essence of great wisdom; the true condition of great self-arising; the fundamental existence of the nature of all objects of knowledge; true awareness; reality itself; identity; great harmony; the heart of the Buddha; the perfection of wisdom; omniscience; the ultimate meaning; emptiness possessing every supreme feature.

It is known as "mind only" because one realizes that all phenomena are mind.

It is called "great central way" philosophy because it is without any center or periphery.

It is called "secret mantra" thought because it is so challenging for everyone to realize.

It is called "the diamond way" because it overcomes all error.

It is called "the body of reality" because you see it to be Buddha nature.

In short, it is without out any limitations brought on by seizing upon it as two distinct things. This is also known as the wisdom of non-duality, identity; great harmony that is free from conceptual complication, Great Seal. This has been a recognition introduction to this.

❋ ❋ ❋ ❋ ❋

In addition to these meditations, you should soar upon rigorous devotion to your spiritual teacher. You should circle upon unending prayers. And you should come to land upon the clear space of your teacher's blessings.

You have recognized this brightness that is not hidden, that is in plain sight, that is not obscured. This is the basis: arrival in the presence of the Great Seal. The path is seeing the fundamental nature of the Great Seal. The result is the determining the Great Seal. So cultivate these practices with joy.

❀ ❀ ❀ ❀ ❀

In this moment you have made the attainment of a human life meaningful. You have started out on the path to liberation and ensured that there will be an end to samsara, this cyclic existence. So it is very important that you meditate with excellence and joy and cultivate this for a long time to come.

You have looked attentively at the resting mind and the moving mind. You have been introduced to them; you have recognized that appearances are mind, that mind is emptiness, that emptiness is spontaneous, that spontaneity is self-liberating. This is the Great Seal. This points a finger toward the enlightened body of reality.

Cultivate your contemplative practice upon this recognition introduction continuously. See this through to completion. Do not just make this an intellectual patch. Take it to heart.

This is the eighth topic for insight meditation.

CHAPTER SEVEN

OURSELVES AND OTHERS

INTRODUCTION

"Oh, my mind, you have sought to work only for your own benefit. You have been doing this for so many countless eons that we cannot even fathom how long it's been. Such profound weariness of body and mind this has resulted in! The only thing you have achieved is your own suffering!"

What would it be like to be another person? To experience their physical, embodied being, their sense of sight, sound, taste, touch. What if we could experience their emotions, their subtle and not-so-subtle responses to the world around them, to other people around them, to the too-often turbulent world that is inside their own heads? And what would it be like to turn our eyes, as another person, back upon ourselves? What would we see when we gazed back at ourselves? What would we think of ourselves from the distant vantage point of another's eyes? And how would we feel about ourselves if we could directly experience our effects upon another person?

Putting ourselves in another's place, "walking a mile in their shoes," is a powerful contemplative practice for exploring the ethical implications of our actions. More subtly, it is a potent way to investigate the ways in which our sense of self can affect our behavior, and thus affect those around us. Most particularly, the imaginative practice of looking back at ourself through another's vision can reveal much, Buddhism says, about the ways that our own selfish behavior, and the potentially destructive emotions and behaviors that are part and parcel of selfishness. It can reveal just how hurtful selfish behavior can be to others, and it can help us to deconstruct that selfishness in an effort to act more compassionately in the world.

Ethics is a key topic of Buddhist meditation, though unlike philosophical writings, contemplative writings offer tools to cultivate ethical behavior in ourselves. These tools include several styles of meditation on ourselves in relation to others, including the meditation presented in this chapter, the famous practice of imaginatively putting oneself in the place of another so that one's happiness becomes theirs, and one heroically takes on their suffering. The source of this practice is the Indian Buddhist work *The Way of the Bodhisattva*. Authored by the poet and philosopher Shantideva in the seventh century, *The Way of the Bodhisattva* presents a comprehensive program for developing bodhicitta, the intense desire to become enlightened so that one may work benevolently to remove the suffering of other living beings. This is the primary aspiration of the bodhisattva, the living being dedicated to enlightenment.

The Way of the Bodhisattva constitutes the most successful overview of Indian Buddhist thought and practice from the later classical period. Between its creation in the seventh century and the waning decades of Buddhism in India, it spawned ten major commentaries. In Tibet, Shantideva's work became the most popular text to use when teaching philosophical ethics in monastic colleges, with dozens of commentaries written over the centuries. Eventually it became one of the few Indian Buddhist philosophical texts to be taught to the public, as popular teachers began to give sermons on its rich teachings to mass audiences. Its chapters cover devotional rituals, fundamental ideas of Buddhist ethics such as charity, patience, and diligence, as well as meditation on the nature of self and philosophical explorations of what exists.

This chapter presents an excerpt from Shenpen Taye's

Notes on Shantideva's Way of the Bodhisattva, which is not so much a commentary as it is a Tibetan prose reworking of the Indian classic. Chapter 8 of *The Way* is a deep consideration of contemplative practice. In it Shantideva presents a gripping meditation in which the mind confronts the mind's propensity for selfishness directly, asking itself, "Can you afford to be selfish?" This passage is one of the most remarkable spiritual exercises of classical Indian Buddhism, a dialogue between different perspectives within a single person, between the multiple "selves" that make up the self.

The Way of the Bodhisattva was composed in verse. And while tradition regards it to be fine poetry in places, the verse form presents challenges to working through the instructions to even get up and running in an already challenging task, imagining oneself as another. This is true today, and it was true in traditional Tibet. Authors such as Shenpen Tayé used *The Way* as a teaching tool to instruct students in the arts of ethical contemplation. One method these teachers used to make the ideas and practices presented in the text more easily accessible was to rewrite Shantideva's work in prose while adding as little as possible in the way of interpretation. These prose versions of the text were popular throughout the nineteenth century, just at the time when *The Way of the Bodhisattva* was emerging as a popular text for sermons to laypeople, who typically had neither the philosophical nor the literary training that monks did. A prose version of the text is especially useful when Shantideva presents a spiritual exercise in the form of a dialogue that readers are intended to speak for themselves. Shenpen Tayé's *Notes* offers a wonderfully readable example of this; the dialogue that the reader is supposed to recite is clearly distinguished from instructions on how to read it. The text to be recited, memorized, and savored in contemplation is approachable and—relatively—easy to make use of.

This chapter presents Shenpen Tayé's *Notes* on fifty verses from the concluding portion of *The Way of the Bodhisattva*'s eighth chapter, which is dedicated to the subject of meditation. This chapter of *The Way* is the fifth in its series of chapters on an important Indian Buddhist program of spiritual development known as the "six perfections": generosity, discipline, patience, diligence, meditation, and wisdom (these are treated, more or less in order, in *The Way of the Bodhisattva*, chapters 3 through 9). Many of the themes treated in these chapters of *The Way* are covered in chapters 3, 5, 6, 7, and 8 here in the present anthology. This is not a coincidence; *The Way* is an important classical source for the foundation practices we have read in chapters 3, 5, and 6.

Shenpen Tayé's *Notes* presents the contemplative practice of imaginatively putting oneself in the place of another person in seven sections. The first section introduces the nature of the practice, and the remaining six provide a script that takes the meditator through a particular emotional challenge. Section one, "Exchanging Oneself for Another: Introduction" (*The Way of the Bodhisattva*, verses 134–140), presents the idea of imagining oneself as another, the reasons why the practice is needed, and the patterns of thought and behavior that it seeks to change. Here Shenpen Tayé identifies what Buddhism takes to be the central challenge to living a fulfilling life; to behaving ethically toward others; and, ultimately, to achieving that radical transformation of thought, feeling, and behavior that makes it possible (or impossible *not*) to live and act for the utmost benefit of other living beings—enlightenment. This challenge is nothing more or less than the very idea that we are single, permanent, substantial selves.

As individuals each of us, according to Buddhism, consider that we are separate from every other person and the environment, so separate that we view all that surrounds us—people, places, things, everything—to be inherently divided into two categories: things that are of direct benefit to our single, permanent, substantial selves, and things that are of direct harm. The Buddhist shorthand for this is the "I," or the self. In contemporary language we might call this the ego, though the term *self* refers to a sense of being that is larger, more comprehensive than the psychoanalytic idea of that part of the mind that is in charge of executive function. This self, the "I" in the Buddhist sense of the word, is our primary means of interacting with the world, and because the I divides the world into things that it deems of benefit to it and things that do harm to it, it is both powerful and destructive. It is destructive because the I is constantly making choices based upon its own self-interest and self-preservation—our self-interest, our self-preservation—to the exclusion of any benefit for everything and everyone else. This might manifest in terms of preferences for trivial items in life, such as certain styles of fashion. It may get more serious, as in the case of rigid adherence to certain ideas that the I sees as either maximally beneficial or harmful to itself. And it may be deadly serious if the I sees a person or people as maximally harmful to itself, and acts to remove that harm—to kill another person or group of people. Because the I always looks out for its own interests, the interests of any other living being are always secondary, and often seen to be the direct cause of threat to the I.

A significant consequence of believing and behaving as if this fiction of the single, permanent, substantial self were real is, according to this Buddhist analysis of self-identity gone wild, that the I is never happy, never satisfied. If everything and everyone is either asset or threat, commodity or deficit, friend or foe, then the I must spend all of its time acquiring what it deems of be of benefit to it and avoiding or destroying what it deems to be harmful. The I never rests from this activity: it knows nothing else. For Buddhism, the I—the complex of thought, feeling, and behavior that sees itself as single, permanent, and uniquely substantial and thus constantly seeks to preserve itself against all that is not it—is the cause of all individual and collective suffering. And so Shenpen Tayé's *Notes* begins: "All the hostility that leads to unhappiness in the world, all of the terrifying things that give rise to sorrow, all of the suffering of body and mind there is—every bit of this originates in clinging to the self, to 'I.'"

How do we begin to work to undo the pervasive destructive capacity of the I upon ourselves and others? The solution proposed here is simple: Give the I away to others. Do exactly what the I does not want, does not expect. Give it to another self, another I, for the benefit of that I, not one's own I. Treat that other I, the other person, as more important than one's own I, one's own being, one's own existence: "Clinging to 'I' causes me to suffer, and it causes other people to suffer. Therefore, in order to remove the harm it does to me and the suffering it causes others, I should give the 'I' to others, and I should cherish others as if they were me." This is the exchange of self and other. This act of giving oneself to another for their benefit is a significant step toward the Buddhist ethical ideals of compassion and love, which we will explore in chapter 8.

After an introductory orientation to the practice and its rationale, Shenpen Tayé presents three practices of exchanging self and other, each dealing with a specific negative emotion: envy, jealousy, and arrogance. Importantly, each also focuses on social status, identifying the emotions we may feel when considering people of inferior, equal, or superior social rank.

"Exchanging Oneself for Another: Envy" (verses 141–146) introduces the first of three topics that the practice is designed to address. Envy here is the sense that while we are unsuccessful in life, others are undeservedly successful. They have achieved what we in fact deserve. We have been wronged by them. This is the theme of the meditation, though here envy can either extend to a general resentment toward others, or it can reduce to a bitterness about one's own state in life, one's fortune or lack thereof. "Exchanging Oneself for Another: Jealousy" (verses 147–150) focuses on people we take to be of equal social status and imagines what we feel when such people reap the benefits of wealth or fame. Finally, "Exchanging Oneself for Another: Arrogance" (verses 151–154) identifies how we feel when considering people whom we feel to be lower on the social ladder.

The trick in each of these is the exchange itself. We, Shenpen Tayé says, envy people of higher social status. We are jealous of people equal to us. And we are arrogant toward those we count as inferior. This is classic Buddhist social psychology; in each situation it is the "I" that drives our perception of reality and our thoughts and behaviors toward others. But what if we put ourselves in the place of the other? What if we look at ourselves from the viewpoint, from the very identity of the other? If we do this, we see ourselves as others see us, and yet we evaluate them exactly as we would them! Instead of being envious of a person of higher rank, I will look back at myself and be envious. Instead of being arrogant toward another, we are another being arrogant right back at us. "I will envy the higher person," says Shenpen Tayé. "I will compete with the equal. I will be arrogant toward the lowly person.

"These are the very nature of destructive emotions, of course. But by putting myself in the place of another, the source where these negative emotions originate switches." And this switch is, according to the logic of the practice, therapeutic; by seeing that others see exactly what we see, we begin, Buddhism argues, to question the truth of our own perspective. How can I be both envious and envied? The practice poses a conundrum for us that we must work through. *The Way of the Bodhisattva* is confident that working through the impossibility of being both the envious and the envied in equal measure is a powerful technique to loosen the hold, however slightly, that the "I" has on our thoughts, emotions, and behaviors, and to begin to value others more highly.

The final three sections of Shenpen Tayé's *Notes* on exchange of self and other offer further techniques to integrate into this suite of spiritual exercises. "Working with the Exchange of Self and Other: Mild Techniques" (verses 155–167) begins with the assumption that the meditator has practiced the preceding exchange of self and other techniques but is perhaps not completely convinced that the practice is actually worth it. How much trouble is the "I"? we ask. Is it really the source of all my problems, and of all the problems I cause to others? Yes, the passage on "mild techniques" answers with measured reason: "Oh, my mind, you have sought to work only for your own benefit. You have been doing this for so many countless eons that we cannot even fathom how long it's been. Such profound weariness of body and mind this has resulted in! The only thing you have achieved is your own suffering! Now you must really work for the benefit of other living beings, using the same effort that you previously made on your own behalf." And if reasoning with the "I" does not work, *The Way of the Bodhisattva* offers a more forceful strategy—the total undoing of the self! "'Mind,'" the practice has you speak to yourself, "you have worked to destroy me by seeking only your own benefit. But that was before. Now I see your faults. This moment is not like before. Now I follow the Buddha's teachings. I have analyzed you well. I see the root of every single one of your faults, Mind. Where will you go now? Your arrogant self-conception will be utterly destroyed!" Yet the result of this practice is not the complete erasure of a sense of self; Buddhism is too pragmatic, too realist for that. Rather, the relative importance of oneself in relation to another is radically upended. Where I thought only of myself, my benefit, my protection, my advancement regardless of everyone and everything else, I now place more emphasis on the well-being of others. This does not come naturally to us, Buddhism reminds us; thus, the need for intense practices such as the exchange of self and other. The ideal result of these exercises is an increased ability to feel compassion and love for others. These Buddhist utopian ideals are the subjects of chapters 8 and 9.

NOTES ON SHANTIDEVA'S WAY OF THE BODHISATTVA (VERSES 134–184), BY SHENPEN TAYÉ

Exchanging Oneself for Another: Introduction

All the hostility that leads to unhappiness in the world, all the terrifying things that give rise to sorrow, all of the suffering of body and mind there is—every bit of this originates in clinging to the self, to "I." This "I" is a great demon, the source of all suffering. What shall I do with it? It is useless! (134)

If I do not get rid of this clinging to "I," I will not be able to be rid of suffering. If you do not let go of the torch in your hand, you will not be able to avoid the fire burning you, for instance. (135)

Clinging to "I" causes me to suffer, and it causes other people to suffer. Therefore, to remove the harm it does to me and the suffering it causes others, I should give the "I" to others, and I should cherish others as if they were me. (136)

"I have come under the power of others": Mind, you must know this with certainty. You will work for the good of all people. Beyond this, Mind, from now on you will not even think about your own needs. (137)

My sight, my hearing, and the others are controlled by another person now, so it is not right to use them for my own purposes. My senses have been sent out for someone else's use, so it is not okay to use them against that person. (138)

So, between me and another person, the other person is the more important person. The clothes on my body—or whatever thing I see that becomes an object of my desire—all of this I will give to other people. If I am not able to give them away because I am overpowered by greed, I will develop a powerful solution for this. Even if all my things are stolen, you, Mind, must give it all away for the benefit of others. (139)

At this moment I accept that I will remove arrogance and other evils of the mind as they relate to people who are subordinate, equal, or superior to me. So now I will identify with someone who is subordinate, someone who is equal, and someone who is superior to me. I will make the other person "me" at each social rank. My mind will have no other thought or doubt. (140)

Exchanging Oneself for Another
at Different Social Ranks

I will exchange with a social inferior to meditate on envy. I will exchange with an equal and meditate on jealousy. I will exchange with a superior to meditate on arrogance.

I will envy the higher person. I will compete with the equal. I will be arrogant toward the lowly person. These are the very nature of destructive emotions, of course. But by putting myself in the place of another, the source where these negative emotions originate switches.

Exchanging Oneself for Another: Envy

Now, I shall meditate on envy. I put myself in another person's place. As that person I think [back upon "me"]:
"That person is admired by the world, while I am not!"
"That person owns things, while I do not."
"That person is praised, while I am insulted."
"That person lives happily, while I suffer." (141)

I think:
"I carry heavy loads and do all sorts of menial labor."
"That one just rests with body and mind at ease."
"That one is known as a 'great' person to the world."
"I am known as lowly and unexceptional. Yet I am the one who is exceptional! So I am the better of us!" (142)

I think:
"What is it to you that I am unexceptional?"
"Anyway, I am not without good qualities. I am exceptional in all kinds of ways. That person is lowlier than many people in the world, and I am better than many people in the world!" (143)

"Perhaps you scorn me because my conduct and my intelligence have slipped. Well, they have waned through the force of my destructive emotions, and I am not capable of fixing this myself. If you look upon me with compassion, you must help me as much as you can! If you do this, I will even accept injury from you." (144)

"But I am not going to be healed by that person, so what reason does that one have to scorn me? That person may have good qualities, but if that one cannot heal me, then they should give their good qualities to me! What is the use to me of seeing good qualities in them?" (145)

"Destitute people engage in harmful activity, and end up living in terrible, poisonous situations. But that person has no compassion for such people! That one publicly boasts of their good qualities to make themselves superior. They want to compete with learned people, so they make people think, 'That smart person (i.e., me) does have faults.'"

To conclude the meditation, you can sum up envy with the following:
    "I have been harmed through many hundreds of rebirths by envy." (146)

Exchanging Oneself for Another: Jealousy

Now I will meditate on jealousy: I shall imagine myself as another person of equal social status, and I will think the following:
    "I will surpass that person [me] in material possessions, or any other thing! I will absolutely achieve greater wealth, reverence, and respect through competition and conflict." (147)

"If my good qualities were known to everyone, no one at all would ever even hear of my opponent's qualities." (148)

"If my many faults, broken virtues, and other such things, were to be concealed, that other person's faults would become apparent. So the honor would go to me, not to them! From now on I would gain and gain riches, while they would not. I would be served by all, while they would not." (149)

"And when that person falls into unwholesome behavior, with their virtues shattered, I shall gaze upon them with delight, and laugh as the whole world shames them. The world will come together to belittle that person!"

To conclude the meditation, you can sum up jealous thinking with the following:

"I have been harmed through many hundreds of rebirths by jealousy." (150)

Exchanging Oneself for Another: Arrogance

Now I will meditate on arrogance. To do so I will think the following:

"It is also well-known that that person [i.e., me] is lowly and filled with destructive emotions. They are competing with me to see who has the best qualities. How can this one possibly be equal to me when it comes to learning, to intelligence, or beauty, class, or wealth? (151)

"Everyone knows of the ways in which we are not equals. And when I hear all these people talking about my good qualities, the hairs on my body stand on end in delight. Such pleasure will I gain from this!" (152)

"If there is even a one-in-a-hundred chance that that person has managed to achieve anything at all, they will be subject to my command. So I will give them enough to survive, but I will use my power to take whatever else they have acquired!" (153)

"And if that person comes to experience any happiness, I will destroy it. I will make sure that they always know much harm and many sorrows!"

To conclude the meditation, you can sum up arrogance with the following:

"I have been harmed through many hundreds of rebirths by arrogance. At this moment I will no longer come under its sway." Remember this. (154)

Working with the Exchange of
Self and Other: Mild Techniques

Oh, my mind, you have sought to work only for your own benefit. You have been doing this for so many countless eons that we cannot even fathom how long it's been. Such profound weariness of body and mind this has resulted in! The only thing you have achieved is your own suffering! (155)

Now you must really work for the benefit of other living beings, using the same effort that you previously made on your own behalf. The teachings of the Buddha are never wrong; eventually you will see the exceptional qualities of this practice of exchanging oneself for another. (156)

Once you have fully completed the work of exchanging yourself for another person, it will then be impossible for you to be without the joy found at the perfect level of Buddhahood. It will be impossible for there to be anything like the present suffering. (157)

Now, you already are attached to the idea that a drop of blood and sperm from others (your parents) is "my body." In just the same way, cultivate the idea that other people are you. (158)

Be the mental scout of that other person and investigate upon your own body. Give everything that seems to be good about your body to others. If it is not given, then take it, and use it to benefit other people. (159)

"I am happy, and others are not. I am high while others are low. I have many helpers who bring benefit to me, while others do not." Shouldn't I be jealous of myself? (160)

So detach yourself from your wealth, and take the sorrows of others' poverty as your own. Analyze your own faults, those actions that are not in accord with the dharma: "What am I doing from this moment on, right now?" (161)

Transform the faults of others into your own as well: "Others' destructive actions—I now perform these. I will also make plain my faults, however small, and fully admit them to others." (162)

"I will shout over my own desire for fame by proclaiming the good qualities of other people. Their fame should surpass my own. I must get rid of my own arrogance, as if I were the humblest servant." (163)

"By nature, I have faults due to my many destructive actions. Even if I do have some fleeting good qualities, I shall not praise those over and above the faults." (164)

In brief, all the work you previously did for your own benefit, and all the various sorts of harm that may have caused other people, should from now on be done for the benefit of others— and any harmful repercussions should fall upon you! (165)

"I shall not cause abuse like someone boasting and praising their own high status. Rather I will act like a bride, modestly striving not to do anything inappropriate. I shall exercise cautiousness owing to my experiences with the perfect teachings, and I will control and settle my sense." (166)

When you are first endeavoring to imagine exchanging yourself for another person, you might say to your mind, "Stay here! If you will not do this, you will be controlled with corrective measures. If you stray from this moral center, Mind, you will be brought under control." (167)

Working with the Exchange of Self and Other: Being Stern with the Mind

"You, Mind! Perhaps you cannot accomplish all of this by means of gently worded instruction? Well, all the destruction that comes from producing a mental orientation toward selfish benefit is entirely reliant upon you. So there is no one else but you who must be defeated!" (168)

"Mind, you have worked to destroy me by seeking only your own benefit. But that was before. Now I see your faults. This moment is not like before. Now I follow the Buddha's teachings. I have analyzed you well. I see the root of every single one of your faults, Mind. Where will you go now? Your arrogant self-conception will be utterly destroyed!" (169)

"Quickly now! Cast off any thought of working only for your own benefit. I have sold you, Mind, to all the other limitless living beings. Do not be sorry for yourself, saying, 'I can't work for other people!' Offer your strength, your ability." (170)

"Mind, you may ask, 'Why are you so unhappy with me and giving me up?' Well, I may slip from this moral center point and fail to exchange myself for another, fail to give you to other living beings. And if I fail to do this, you will surely hand me over to the terrifying demons of hell, of this there is no doubt." (171)

"And, Mind, you might ask, 'What harm have I ever done to you that resulted in such a thing?' Well, you've done this before. Many times have you handed me over to the demons of hell, and long have I suffered there. So now I have remembered those old grudges, and I will destroy you and your self-interested thoughts." (172)

"If I wish to strive for some way to achieve happiness, I should not work to please myself. If I wish to protect myself from all terrors, I must always protect other living beings from all terrors." (173)

Working with the Exchange of Self and Other: Being Stern with the Body

The more that this body, which is by nature conflicted, is coddled, or completely sheltered, the more it becomes easily affronted, and eventually falls into being unable to cope with even the slightest distress. (174)

You may ask, "What kind of deterioration can lead to such an intense fall?" Well, the desires of one who has fallen so far cannot be fully satisfied even with everything on this earth. So what person can give them what they desire? (175)

Such a being has no power and desires so much, so destructive emotions such as hatred or envy overpower them, and their mind deteriorates. Yet the person who lives with no regard for body or wealth knows no end to prosperity. (176)

So I will give no chance for my body's desires to grow. The things that do not come to be captivating objects of desire are the best things. Such things are, first of all, easy to achieve, they don't result in attachment, and in the end, they don't result in sorrow when they are gone from you. But you might say, "That is the case for material wealth, but surely this body is to be cherished!" (177)

Well, what is this body like? In the end it will become dust, that is its final state. Even now the body itself is inert; it is powered by something else. For it is animated by consciousness. This bodily form is inherently polluted. It is the source of all fears, and because of this it is unbearable. Given all this, why would you cling to it as "you"? (178)

What am I to do with a machine like this, no matter if it is alive or dead! What difference is there between this body and a clump of dirt? Why are you not bringing this arrogance, which thinks, "This thing is 'me,'" to an end? It is pitiful. (179)

You have persistently treasured this body, and by this have amassed so much useless suffering. On behalf of this body, you both loved and hated, and what have you achieved with all this effort just for something that is like a piece of wood? (180)

"I might lovingly protect it so, or it might be devoured by vultures or foxes. Either is possible. It does not love me, and it does not hate the vulture. So why do I love this body as 'me'?" (181)

"It is not angry when it is insulted, and it is not glad when it is praised. If this body knows neither of these, for what possible reason do I wear myself out on it? I should learn to consider that this is meaningless." (182)

"And even though my body does not know them, there are people who love this body, who find it attractive. Now you might say that these people are friends. But everyone with a body is attached to their own bodies and finds it agreeable. So why would I be joyous on their behalf as much as for myself? It would make sense to find joy regarding every person who has a body." (183)

"So I will give up cherishing and hating for my own sake and dedicate this body to benefiting other people. It does have many faults and has known many sorrows, but I will use it for the task at hand, a requirement of the job." (184)

CHAPTER EIGHT

COSMIC LOVE

INTRODUCTION

"If you collected all the tears [your mother] has wept because she was so forlorn over your death, it would exceed a billion rivers."

This chapter presents a meditation on love. The kind of love described here is modeled upon an ideal kind of love that, within the world of classic Buddhist teachings, at least, a mother feels for her child. Mothers, in this ideal sense, give everything in their lives, up to and including life itself, for their children. Here mothers feel this love innately, without forethought. They act upon this love of their children without hesitation, doing whatever it takes to be of benefit to their children. In this love, no child is unworthy, and no sacrifice is too great.

And as with mothers, so with all of us; we should—and we can—dedicate our lives to other people, and a crucial emotion to enact this dedication is love. The meditation on cosmic love here is a tool for, once again, cultivating that most utopian of Buddhist ideas, that humans can see beyond their own self-interest and live for the benefit of others. Living beings who have pushed this possibility to the limit are called Buddhas.

The passage on cosmic love translated here is from a twentieth-century text entitled *A Short Overview of Buddhism for Beginners That Is Easy to Keep in Mind*. Its author, Ngawang Yönten Gyatso (1928–2002), was a prominent

Buddhist teacher in northeastern Tibet. He belonged to the Jonang School of Tibetan Buddhism, a tradition that has its roots in twelfth-century southwestern Tibet. The distinctive philosophical systems of the Jonang Tradition did not always enjoy political favor, so much so that they were run out of western Tibet only to find secure place in the northeast. But despite their unique philosophy, they promoted a form of contemplative ethics that is shared across traditions. Although Gyatso was active relatively recently, the practice he presents here is very old in Buddhism. In fact, *A Short Overview of Buddhism for Beginners* contains instructions that can be found throughout the foundation practice literature, which we were introduced to in chapters 3, 5, 6 and, although only indirectly related, chapter 7's practice of exchanging self and other. With this final installment on love from the foundation practices, we see a common contemplative program that is shared among all the major schools of Buddhism, including the Geluk, Kagyu, Sakya, Nyingma, and Jonang. Reflections on living and dying, finding inner calm, cultivating a wider perspective, learning to see ourselves as others see us, and cultivating love: this set of contemplative practices is foundational to the entire tradition of Tibetan Buddhist meditation.

The section translated here is a practice for cultivating feelings of love and compassion toward other people. This is typically taught in conjunction with the exchange of self and other practice that we encountered in chapter 7, for the two practices each ask the practitioner to reimagine the relationship between oneself and other people in radical ways, using intense forms of contemplative imagination.

The meditation on love is founded upon the notion of rebirth. This takes the doctrine of rebirth to a logical extreme. If we have been reborn many times—effectively an infinite number of times—and if those rebirths have been as different people, then we have, the logic goes, been born as everyone. This spiritual exercise takes the idea of rebirth and runs with it, challenging our capacity to imagine the bond between self and other. The system intentionally confuses "I" with other in a way that is reminiscent of the previous practice, but with an exponential twist. I have, in some sense, remained "I" throughout the countless lifetimes I have lived. And "I" have been someone else. The same goes for every other person. And if both I and others have been reborn as "another," then we have had countless chances to have different relationships with each other. You and I might never have met in a particular rebirth. Or you and I could be in the same state, or city, or town, passing by each other on the street. Or we could be friends in one lifetime. We could also be related in a given lifetime. I could be your brother, your sister, your cousin, aunt, uncle . . . your parent . . . your mother in just a single one of those countless lifetimes, all because I have been reborn as "another" and you have been reborn as another. And if we extend this back from the present lifetime, back an uncountably large number of lifetimes, back infinitely from this moment, then there is no relationship between "you" and "I" in which you and I have not participated, and for an infinite amount of recurrences—and the same goes for every other person in existence.

This is a powerful extension of the notion of rebirth. It moves logically, within the system, from a doctrine of individual continuation between successive material and immaterial states to a doctrine of complete interrelation. Taking the infinite view, everyone has been related to everyone else in every conceivable configuration, including that of mother and child.

To make this admittedly abstract idea more vivid, the practice asks the meditator to imagine an increasingly larger and more varied cast of living beings. The practice begins with a goal that is humbler than love: impartiality. This is simply treating people equally, regardless of our perception of their value or lack thereof for our own interests. Developing some measure of impartiality is a prerequisite for that more powerful and dynamic feeling, love. *A Short Overview of Buddhism for Beginners* starts by characterizing the ideal form of love as a mother's love for her children. This is a vivid passage, meant to inspire a heightened emotional state as one moves through the meditation that follows. If we recall, or perhaps imagine, the personal sacrifice that our mother has made on our behalf, so *A Short Overview* wagers, we will be more emotionally receptive to considering the virtues of others as we begin to imagine them as having been our mother in past lives.

Beginning with "Meditation on a Mother's Love," the meditation proper provides a script for the practitioner to work with. As in previous chapters, this script is best approached in several passes. First, read through the entire meditation, noting major themes and imaginative cues. Then return to the beginning and work slowly through the individual practices. Each deserves time and patience in order to settle in our thoughts and emotions. And each calls for a distinct scope of reference as the practices move from personal to cosmic proportions.

Even though the logic of the mother's cosmic love is temporal, the meditations are more spatial in character; we move from the local to the global to the cosmic to the universal, along the way picking up different kinds of beings who dwell in these realms rather than specific people who have been our mothers in past lives. We begin imagining the care and kindness that our own mother has shown us in this lifetime. Then we move to family members, imagining the close-knit community that has supported us in this life. We then begin to expand the range of living beings who have loved us, and who are therefore worthy of love. This next practice begins considering other people who might live in your town, your region, or your country. Significantly, this meditation then takes a radical step away from humans to animals; in the doctrine of rebirth, any kind of living being can be reborn as any other type of living being. Animals, therefore, are worthy of all the attention and respect that humans merit in this system. (This extension of the ethics of love to animals has significant implications for our treatment of animals, which some Buddhists express through adopting and promoting a vegetarian diet; this is usually treated in separate works dedicated specifically to dietary ethics rather than integrated into meditation instructions, but it is worth noting here that both meditations on love and dietary practices such as vegetarianism draw on the same Buddhist philosophical ideas of karma and rebirth.)

Finally, the practice leaps into other realms, asking the practitioner to imagine a Buddhist cosmos, with its world-anchoring mountain, Mount Meru, and the many types of beings who adorn its slopes and surrounding celestial environment. Ultimately, we extend our meditation on love all the way from our own mothers to every single living being in every possible universe throughout the infinite expanse of space and time. In this we are perhaps imagining, however imperfectly and momentarily, how the Buddha looks upon beings with infinite, cosmic love.

A SHORT OVERVIEW OF
BUDDHISM FOR BEGINNERS
THAT IS EASY TO KEEP IN MIND,
BY NGAWANG YÖNTEN GYATSO

Cultivating Impartiality

Now we will speak of love. Initially we need to integrate impartiality into our contemplative experience. If we do not do so, our meditations on love, compassion, and so forth can fall into being one-sided. Our love and compassion will not be pure if that happens. So we will train our minds to be impartial.

Impartiality means letting go of both our hatred of our enemies and our affection for our friends and relatives. For all living beings we act without bias, without attachment or hatred. We give these up with an impartial mind. This is called "impartiality."

At the moment we are very attached to our father, our mother, and our relatives—to anyone on our own side. And we foster intolerable hatred toward enemies, or people on the other side. This is a fault, and it is due to the fact that we have not analyzed things for ourselves.

In previous lives, those who are enemies at this moment have been our friends. They have been our dear companions. They have looked after us with goodwill. The benefits they have provided have been immeasurable. And the people we currently call Father, Mother, and so forth have in previous lives been our enemies. They have been among the many who have done us harm! Noble Katyayana says, "That one eats his father's flesh. He strikes his mother. He keeps his enemies, with their wicked deeds, right upon his lap! And his wife is gnawing on his, her husband's, bones. I scoff at these scenes from samsara!"

Similarly, father, mother, and son are intimately connected. The love and affection one feels for the other is inconceivable. If they experience suffering or any undesirable thing at all, our pain is immense. But who among those that we consider our enemies at this moment has not also been our father, our mother? If we were to use our ingenuity to understand what they are thinking, it would not be difficult to become their friends.

So think to yourself as much as possible: "I must live with boundless equanimity, free of biased desires." You must practice impartiality before you practice love, according to Master Kamalashila, as he teaches this in his work, *The Stages of Meditation.*

Mothers' Love

After this, we first cultivate love. Send your thoughts out to each living being in the entire cosmos. Wherever you go, the sky is endless. Just so, the cosmos is without limit. And every single sort of living being is spread uninterruptedly throughout the cosmos.

And there is not a single one of those living beings who, at one time or another, has not been your mother or your father. The *Letter to a Student* says about mothers, "There is no land in which they have not lived. There is no living being who has not slept in their bellies."

This cyclic existence is without beginning. The rebirths I've undergone are without beginning. The series of births and deaths proceed continuously, so there is no place, nor is there a body in which I have not been born. And since there is no one who has not also slept in the belly of that living being, there is not a single living being who has not been my own mother, my own father. Nagarjuna says, "You would run out of earth trying to count the total number of mothers with juniper berries."

Living beings have been your mother time and again. Again and again, they have extended immense help to you. Such is the kindness of mothers. So you must repay this kindness. In the same way each person has been your mother, so the limitless living beings, as infinite as space, have been your mother. And not just once or twice! They have been your mother again and again. They have extended vast support to you time and again. As it is said, "Everyone has been your mother. You have drunk the milk of your mothers, and even the ocean does not compare to how much milk that is! And everyone has been your father. The number of horses and elephants he has given you would overflow even the god Brahma's world." Similarly, your abbot, spiritual master, mother and father, your elder and younger brothers, your sisters, your friends, your relatives, your enemies, demons, animals, denizens of hell, gods, humans, everyone: each of these beings has been your mother or father in some lifetime, all through the power of karma.

Now, as we have said, living beings filling the ends of space have served as your mother and your father. However, as a scripture says, "Since times long past, there has been some person who has been your father, your mother, your brother, your sister, your teacher, your abbot, your master. But since we are not spiritual masters, this is very difficult for us to see." Those people who have been my mother or my father—I cannot see them with the all-knowing wisdom of the Buddhas.

So I must call to mind again the certainty that "all living beings have been my mother." I must say to myself, "My current root mother is the mother who gave birth to me in this life." This mother has been so kind to me. She has supported me with food, with labor that is so beneficial to me, and made sure I do not eat unhealthy foods.

When I was born, the karmic winds of existence tumbled head over foot. When I was led through the birth canal, I experienced such pain, as if a strong-armed person grabbed me by the feet and slammed me against a wall! And when I was dragged through the pelvic canal, I experienced pain as if I were clutched with a pair of iron tongs. And if the birth canal is too small, and you cannot emerge, well, either the mother, or the child, or both mother and child will die. And even if you do not die, you experience pain that is almost like death.

The Love Shown to Master Orgyen by his Mother

Master Orgyen tells us the following:

> A mother with child puts one foot,
> Into the land of the dead.
> Every joint except for her jaw,
> Separates in the mother's body!

Yet you, the child, knows nothing of her labors. You are as bloody as a vampire—this being that the mother holds on to with all ten fingers, all out of motherly love. She embraces you in the warmth of her body. She provides you milk. She prepares your food. She cleans up your filth with her own hands. She sustains you with an affectionate attitude. She looks out for you, protects you with the eye of love. She calls out to you with a sweet voice. She gives you praise even when there is no cause for praise. She talks about your good qualities even if you do not have any. She keeps you safe from fire, water, or cliffs. She protects you from becoming afflicted by hot and cold weather. When you are hungry and thirsty, she provides food and drink. She keeps you content through all manner of tricks. She cannot bear to be apart from you. She holds you so dear that her heart falls to pieces.

She teaches you everything you do not know, such as how to eat properly. How to walk. How to sit. How to talk. How to behave. How to watch out for harmful people. How to look out for your family. All of these she teaches for her child's—for your—benefit. When you grow big, she gives whatever wealth she has to you, her child. Even if she gave you all the jewels and wealth of three thousand worlds, she would not think that it was enough.

"My mother is the only one who provides all of this benefit to me. I understand the work she has undertaken as a mother; now I must practice showing her thanks."

Meditation on a Mother's Love

Just as Master Orgyen tells us, my mother cultivates love for me, so I will meditate on her love as follows:

"It would be perfect if this immensely kind person were content while she was a mother, and happy in all other states of existence. In previous lives this person, currently my mother, has been born as a butcher, or many other kinds of people. She has protected me with ill-gotten food. For her, such work has been endless. To protect her child, she has endured countless types of death herself, more than all the atoms in this great earth.

"If you piled up all the clothes she has ever worn or the jewelry she has put on throughout her lives, it would be higher than the great Mount Meru. If you amassed all the milk that she has produced, it would be greater than four oceans. If you collected all the tears she has wept because she was so forlorn over your death, it would exceed a billion rivers.

"For the benefit of her child, she never gave a single glance at destructive behavior. For the benefit of her child, she never shied away from trouble. She never gave a glance at gossip, but always worked exclusively for the benefit of her child, for me. She undertook all of the beneficial labor just for this one, for me."

Cultivating Love for Family

In his *Letter to a Student*, Candragomin says, "If someone in your family were to sink into this cyclic existence, looking like someone falling into a deep chasm, migrating between birth and death, and if you were to leave them without acknowledging them in order to save yourself, there would be nothing more disgraceful!

"Just so, all living beings migrate between birth and death. So not acknowledging them, but rather leaving every one of those mothers who have extended inexpressible kindness to you to sink into the ocean of suffering—well, there is nothing more shameful than that!"

Cultivating Love for Other People and Animals

Now, the meditation on love developed by Geshé Jayulwa and Nartangpa advises that we should begin with the idea that all living beings have been each of our mothers, just like my present root mother. Then we should expand our range of meditation beyond our own mothers to larger and larger regions. This is how beginners should meditate on love, because it treats the most important points of this meditation.

In the region in which you live, there are three different kinds of people: friends, enemies, and people in between. And there are three kinds of animals: land-dwelling animals, soil-dwelling animals, and animals in between. And there are three kinds of hungry ghosts, and demons, and spirits: powerful, weak, and in between.

All these beings have been your mother and your father throughout innumerable lifetimes. Apply the previous contemplation of your mother to them as well, considering the kindness they have shown, and so forth.

Now expand your range of thought again, this time to your country. If you are in Tibet, first meditate on the three types of living beings living in the whole of Tibet. Then expand eastward to China. Then south to India. Then west to Kashmir. Then north to Mongolia, Tajikistan, and so forth. Meditate on the three sorts of people living in all those countries. And there are living beings upon the lands of each of the eight great and four small continents. And there are living beings who are underground, or living out unfortunate destinies, as well as others elsewhere. Extend out, meditating on each of these as we have demonstrated.

Cultivating Love for Creatures on Mount Meru—the World Mountain

Then there are the gods of the four great royal lineages who live upon the four terraces of the great world mountain, Meru. There are the gods who live on the summit in the Heaven of the Thirty-Three Gods. And there are those at the foot of the shorelines along the corners, where the leaders of the demigods live. Meditate as before on every being who lives in each of these places.

From there move to the seven golden mountains, the iron wall surrounding them, and the shores along it. Gods, mischievous spirits, and animals live under and around the shore. And at the outskirts of the world mountain Meru, there are seven lakes, and in the outermost lake live serpents, demigods, and animals of every sort, all mixed together. Cultivate love toward all these living beings as before.

There are three sorts of animals who have magical powers. Garuda birds fly through the sky. Kinnara beasts walk upon the earth. Serpent deities dwell underground or underwater. Meditate individually on love for these living beings.

Cultivating Love for Celestial Beings in the Cosmos

That meditation stretches from underground up to the vast golden surface, and from the outer iron wall up to the Heaven of the Thirty-Three Gods. Above that are the celestial realms called the Limitless Realm, the Joyous Realm, the Realm Where Emanations Are Enjoyed, and the Realm of Controlling Other's Emanations. Meditate on love for all beings in these realms, one by one.

Then above that there are the three realms where the beings experience the first meditative absorption. These are named God Brahma's Realm, Praise in the Presence of Brahma, and Great Brahma. Each of these is itself the size of a single one of the lower world realms. Expand your meditation outward to these.

In these realms of the cosmos that have physical form there are only deities living; none of the other five types of living beings (hell beings, hungry ghosts, animals, humans, or demigods) live there. In each of these cosmic realms only a particular type of celestial being resides [. . . lines 234.1– 235.1 not translated].

Cultivating Love for All Living Beings throughout Space

Taken together, these and other physical realms amount to one billion worlds—a galaxy. You must expand your meditation to these, and even to the innumerable living beings who live beyond this in realms without physical form. Meditate upon every living being of every type in all cosmic realms.

Beyond this cosmic realm of one galaxy there are innumerable other galaxies—and that's just to the east! Let me give an example of how many this is: Pack just a single galaxy entirely full of mustard seeds. Then take one mustard seed at a time from that system and put it in a single galaxy to the east. You would eventually run out of mustard seeds. But the galaxies running east would never run out! Were you to do this again in another direction, you would run out of mustard seeds, but the galaxies would never run out. Try it in any another direction, and the same thing would happen. Keep doing this forever, for endless eons; the world realms would never run out. And every single one of these world realms is filled with the six sorts of living beings.

Understand that every single one of these living beings has been your mother. Bring to mind the kindness that they have shown you. Cultivate love for each one of them, just as we have explained.

And the galaxies to the east are just the beginning. Throughout every single direction there are galaxies just like that. Space is infinite in every direction. And the entirety of this space is filled with worlds. And each of these worlds is filled with living beings of all sorts.

And each of these beings has been your mother and your father. And the number of times each of these living beings has been your mother or your father is inconceivable. And in each of these lives they have benefited you in every way. They have cleared away harm in every way.

"These mothers of the ages must be content. They must be happy. I will make effort without equal to ensure their contentment and happiness!"

Think this as you cultivate love for them.

The Benefits of Love

"If," says a scripture, "a person in a perfect realm who had upheld virtue for an eon were, even for one moment, to practice love, this would be their most holy act. If a person in this same perfect realm were to engage in sin with body, speech, and mind, they would plunge into the worst states of existence. And yet, if they practiced a single loving thought, they would immediately be purified in wisdom. A bodhisattva who is born in a negative state of existence should have no fear, should not be concerned. For they may fall to a realm of sin, but they will be purified through love—even of a simple headache!"

A single moment of compassionate love, according to one scripture, is better than giving a gift to every single person. "For the person who cultivates love as their dharma is contented," says the Buddha.

The *Verses on Dharma* say,

> Someone may give a thousand offerings each month,
> And they may do that for a hundred years,
> But they cannot compare with someone
> Who, even for a moment, loves living beings.

Whoever gives with loving compassion, according to the *Ornament for Scriptures*, produces more wealth, love, and care. And through that they themselves are happy because of their work. "There is no way to please the Buddha other than making living beings happy," says another scripture.

In fact, the best way to achieve any merit for yourself is to love. "You might give three hundred containers of food every day, three times a day," Master Nagarjuna tells us. "But even a moment of love will bring you more merit than this." He also says, "You will delight both gods and humans, and in turn they will protect you, keeping you safe from such things as poison or violence. You will have a happy outlook and many happy experiences. You will achieve your aims without effort. Not only will you become liberated, but you will also be reborn in the Brahma's celestial realm. These are the eight great benefits of love."

Summary

"When you cast your eyes upon people, look upon them with the eyes of love," says *The Way of the Bodhisattva*.

"Guests from far away, those who have been ill for a long time, aging parents—when you show love for such people, it is like meditating on the essential meaning of emptiness and compassion," says Lord Atisha.

Even the Buddha, according to the scripture, traveled to the Heaven of the Thirty-Three Gods to teach the dharma to his mother, all to repay the kindness she had shown him. "A child might put their mother and father on each shoulder," thought the Buddha, "and carry them all the way around the earth. But even this act of service would not be sufficient to repay their kindness. If I were to introduce them to the dharma, that would effectively repay them." Reflect continuously on what the Buddha is conveying here.

There are different ways to contemplate the various parts of these meditations on love. You must make them work best for your own style of thinking.

CHAPTER NINE

OPEN MIND, VAST MIND

INTRODUCTION

This chapter moves from formal meditation instructions to a more relaxed style of advice about meditation. The topics vary, though the common thread is mind, specifically the naturalness of the mind in meditation. These lively and humane meditations on the inherently positive potential of the human mind were written by one of Tibet's most famous meditation teachers, Patrul Rinpoche (1808–1887). Patrul's *Naturally Liberated Meditation: Profound Methods for Buddhahood—the Ultimate Great Perfection*, contains a dozen or so pieces of advice on the contemplative life, offered in disarmingly direct poetry and prose. Patrul was deeply learned in formal methods of introducing contemplative practice. In fact, he is the author of the most famous work on the foundation practices of the last two centuries in Tibet, *The Words of My Perfect Teacher*. Much that is taught in that work will be familiar to those who have read chapters 3, 5, 6, 7, and 8 here.

In what follows, Patrul blends poetry and a lyrical prose to emphasize that, however challenging we may find meditation at times, our minds are naturally clear and aware. For him this means that we have all that we need to begin meditating, to develop a meditation practice, and to be successful in the work of reducing suffering for ourselves and others through meditation. This is a genuinely positive outlook on existence, and on the capacity of human beings to employ their key strength—the very fact that we are aware, thinking beings—in order to improve everything from our emotions and behaviors to our social and environmental worlds. This deeply positive view of mind is a hallmark of Patrul's tradition, the Nyingma School of Tibetan Buddhism, though it has its roots in classical Indian Buddhist views of "Buddha nature," the idea that every living being has the innate potential to achieve enlightenment. Patrul's view of mind is akin to the notion of "ordinary awareness" of the Kagyu School, which we encountered in chapter 6. Distinctive is the emphasis that Patrul places on the natural ease of experiencing mind as clear, vivid awareness in meditation. There is, paradoxically, nothing to "do" in meditation here. The contemplative process involves letting go, letting the mind come to rest, to simply *be*, rather than forcefully training the mind to *do* something.

There are twelve pieces here, each of which asks the contemplative practitioner to understand, and then to experience this letting go in slightly different terms. "Mind Just as It Is" begins with a litany of names for mind, characterized here as both the source and the goal of enlightenment. Mind in the mundane sense is the thoughts and emotions that buzz throughout our heads every day, from morning until night and into our dreams. It is the cause of our suffering as well as others' suffering, as Shenpen Tayé's *Notes on the Way of the Bodhisattva* sought to make clear. Yet "mind" taken in an elevated sense is enlightenment itself, the supreme goal of Buddhism itself. The trick here, Patrul wants to make clear, is that both minds are in fact the same thing. Because of this, we can name the mind with any and all of the epithets for the experience of enlightenment. It is "the mind of all Buddhas of the three times," and that mind is, in an essential sense, our mind.

Throughout these teachings Patrul often speaks with a sense of calm humor, a sort of unruffled matter-of-factness about mind that belies the immensity of what he comes back to again and again: mind is always clear and vivid awareness, which is enlightenment itself. And if you realize this, well, Patrul assures us, the world is still here in all its vivid

particularity: "If you realize it in the morning, you are awakened in the morning. If you realize it in the evening, you are
awakened in the evening."

"Unfabricated Mind" highlights another key term that is
used to try to get at this admittedly slippery notion. *Unfabricated* here means working without a rigid intellectual frame,
tightly scheduled procedures, and definite goals. Patrul's
ideal meditation is relatively loose here compared with the
scripted meditations, or even the calm and focus meditations
of chapter 4: "When your mind is agitated, thinking of one
thing now and some other thing in the next moment, let your
mind be loose and free. In this loose and free state, be both
alert and mindful of this activity of thinking of one thing one
moment and another the next. Remain in this loose and free
state without getting lost in distraction." Looseness. Freedom. These are the hallmarks of Patrul's "unfabricated" contemplative style.

This is not to say that meditation is not challenging. Patrul
is acutely aware of the careful balance between effort and
laxity that is called for here. "The Mind's Faults" points out
some of the pitfalls that practitioners can stumble into when
engaged in this work. Self-doubt, fear of failure, lack of confidence in one's own capacity to understand. His answer:
trust your mind. On what grounds? "A Discussion of Freeing
the Mind" offers an answer: "Your mind has existed in you
since the beginning. It is not something you lose or find. It is
not something that exists or does not exist. This mind that
you've had since the beginning thinks when you think, does
not think when you don't think. This itself is the mind." And
here Patrul moves between mind as unenlightened and mind
as enlightened, for, as he has said, they are in essence one and
the same.

A key term in this passage is *emptiness. Emptiness* is a
fundamental term in Buddhist philosophy with several meanings. It can refer generally to impermanence, the idea that
nothing and no one lasts forever. It can refer to the lack of a
single, independent self, or identity, in either people or things.
Another term for this latter meaning is *no-self. Emptiness*

can also be used as a shorthand term for the Buddhist idea that, while we perceive objects to be separate from the perceiver (i.e., our own mind and senses), in reality the perceiving subject and the perceived object are not different. They are the same complex of immaterial and material forces. As we say in chapter 6 on insight meditation, Buddhism cares about this because it says that the subject-object distinction is a primary cause of human suffering; our selves, believing themselves to be independent, constantly search for objects, which they also believe to be independent, separate from us. This process is ultimately disappointing, frustrating us perpetually, because we can never get enough objects "out there" to make the mind "in here" feel satisfied. This is desire. So emptiness in this case is an analysis of how minds carry out a false, "dualistic" separation of subject and object, which leads to desire, which leads to suffering.

It is this notion of emptiness that Patrul highlights. His remedy for this is common throughout these teachings: let the mind be as it is. "Letting it be" means doing away with the separation of experience and its objects or doing away with an exclusive focus upon one type of experience as *the* real, authentic experience and another as incorrect, inauthentic: "Some meditators do not look at that which is doing the thinking, the mind. They look a great deal at the objects of their thinking, at their belongings, or at the ground, or at rocks. This is not the correct viewpoint. This is a dualistic viewpoint. Let that which thinks be just as it is, and then look." And in letting it be and looking, one finds, Patrul affirms, an awareness that is always there. And, as he has already said, this is an awareness, a cognitive energy that is without an object, where the thinking subject and the thought object are not two separate things, but rather one, empty and aware.

The larger part of this section consists of a long list of the kinds of syndromes, negative feedback loops, that contemplative practitioners might find themselves entangled in. This repays repeat readings, and slow appreciation, as practitioners ask themselves how each of these might highlight something in their own experience.

"An Instruction on the Self-Liberation of Confusion, which Turns Toxin into Remedy" continues with the theme of emptiness, yet it is simpler in form than the preceding sections. These verses offer a chance to contemplate a basic set of negative emotional states and behaviors, each verse highlighting a single experience: greed, hatred, anger, laziness, distraction, delusion, and conceit. "An Instruction on the Self-Liberation of Disturbing Emotions" follows the same pattern, this time treating suffering, destructive emotions, hatred, conceit, attachment, envy, delusion, torpor, anxiety, and, as a concluding set, the "three poisons," the triad of negative cognitive and emotional states of greed, hatred, and delusion, which Buddhism emphasizes as the root causes of much, if not all, of human suffering. Key to overcoming these states is focus, or non-distraction, a skill that brings us back to calm meditation in chapter 3. Focus allows the practitioner to identify, observe, and analyze the workings of negative emotions and, ultimately, to reduce their impact on one's experience by understanding that they do not constitute oneself, that they can be transformed into more positive states of experience.

"Remarks on Possible Experiences When Working with the Mind" and "Ascertaining the Basic State of Mind" continue the "let it be" theme, this time pointing out specific sorts of experiences the meditator may have: "At times a meditator's mind may come to not think about anything; it is just empty and vivid. In moments like this, do not try to fix it. Just let it be vivid in and of itself." At other times your thoughts and emotions may be "dark, vague, vacant, and unable to find clarity." Yet rather than resist these states as "negative," Patrul instructs the practitioner to maintain an even state, as one would when in "positive" states. Let it be. And in letting the mind be, Patrul advises, we build not just our capacity to experience calm, clear, vivid awareness in meditation, but also the confidence that we are actually capable of building that capacity in the first place, because we have all that we need, right here in our own minds: "You do not need to change a thing, for this mindful awareness encompasses everything, just like the sky."

"Performing the Four Practices on the Path of the Bodhisattva" highlights another set of basic human activities, namely moving, sitting, sleeping, and eating. In each of these, Patrul urges contemplative practitioners not to forget their meditation experience; keep the focus on mind, and on maintaining supple and relaxed control of one's thoughts and emotions. The final three pieces in Patrul's collection of meditation advice emphasize a point made earlier, especially in chapter 7; it is important, according to Buddhism, to learn meditation from an experienced teacher. Buddhism is a tradition that values personal instruction; there is no better teaching method for contemplative practice, Patrul reaffirms, than mentorship. "Ask people who are learned," he counsels, "so you may resolve your doubts, without spinning your head in circles!"

NATURALLY LIBERATED MEDITATION, BY PATRUL RINPOCHE

Mind Just as It Is

Unmoving from the pure body of reality,
Ever awakened from the root causes of existential error,
Samantabhadra—the deity All Good—may I quickly
  realize your mind,
Just as it is, with no faults at all.

If you, spiritual heirs, wish to gain enlightenment,
This wandering beggar, Old Dog Patrul,
Will put some authentic advice in verse.
Diligent students, I ask you, take this into your practice.

Emptiness, the body of dharma.
The personal deity of all master adepts
The mind of all Buddhas of the three times.
The life root of all personal deities.
The heart-blood of the muses.
The foundation of all protectors of the dharma.
The essence of all the exoteric and esoteric scriptures.
The quintessence of all esoteric words of spiritual power.

[These are all the same.] They are taught Great Seal, Great Perfection, or Great Middle traditions as a direct instruction, which is this: The body of reality is inseparable from your own mind. Simply know this, and everything becomes the Sovereign King [Samantabhadra, also known as], the Great Seal of reality.

If you realize it in the morning, you are awakened in the morning.

If you realize it in the evening, you are awakened in the evening.

And in these magnificent terms, there is magnificent meaning, which is just this:

When the empty, unfabricated mind is left just as it arises, it is called nothing else but itself.

Men and women, if you wish to realize the correct spiritual viewpoint without error, just let your mind be. Let it be vivid and clear in a unfabricated, empty state.

And if you have a thought, let that thought, too, be just as it is, without changing it. If you are not thinking of anything, leave it without changing it just as it is, not thinking of anything.

In short, leave your mind just as it emerges, without changing anything.

Do not change anything. Don't take anything away, don't add anything. Whatever happens, leave it just as it happens, without changing it. Don't put your mind right here, and the source of spiritual view over there. Leave the viewer and the thinker just where they are, without changing them, simply as one's mind. Don't put your mind right here, and search for the source of meditation over there.

Leave without fabrication the one doing the meditation, just as it is, as your own mind. You search for your mind, but you can't locate it, for it is empty from the beginning. Even though you search, you don't need to, for the searcher is your mind itself.

If you think, "Do I understand or not? Is this the spiritual view to be seen or not? Is it this or not?"—whatever you think, let that thinker be without changing it, just as it is. If you recollect something good or bad, fine or ugly, happy or sad, without accepting or rejecting these, let that recollector be without changing it, just as it is. If desire arises, or if no desire arises, let that arising be without changing it, just as it is.

Oral lineage says, "Unfabricated ground of being is the Great Seal. Unfabricated spiritual path is the Great Middle. Unfabricated result is the Great Perfection."

Unfabricated Mind

Now I'll clear up a few issues about this term "unfabricated."

When your mind is agitated, thinking of one thing now and some other thing in the next moment, let your mind be loose and free. In this loose and free state, be both alert and mindful of this activity of thinking of one thing one moment and another the next. Remain in this loose and free state without getting lost in distraction.

When subtle thoughts pass through your consciousness quickly, your basic awareness appears and disappears. When this happens, bring this awareness together. Let it be bright and vivid. Rest your mind in this state, limpid and lucid.

When your mind is lethargic, dull, or depressed, don't grasp at bliss and clarity. Just let these thoughts exist in their own place. Do not try to fix them. Rest.

If your mind is happy or sad, just let that happy or sad mind be, just as it is. Don't wander, just rest there. If you are elated, or feeling rich and proud, or someone offers you admiration, don't give in to following the demon of elation up to the heavens. Keep your head bowed and your eyes low. Let your body and mind remain at rest.

If you are sick, suffering, or robbed, if you are verbally abused, a victim of bad circumstances, or starving, don't bow your head. Don't lose your radiant face. Don't cry. Let feelings of joy spread. Rest with a smile on your face.

The Mind's Faults

Now I'll present the mind's faults:

Men and women who meditate may think that they do not know how to recognize the mind. They become depressed, weep, and shed many tears.

There is no need to be depressed! There is no reason you cannot understand your mind! Let that very one who thinks there is no way to understand how to recognize the mind be itself, just at it is. That very one is the mind.

Some men and women who meditate say that it is difficult to develop recognition of the mind. It is not difficult at all. The problem is not knowing meditation.

You don't need to search for meditation.

You don't have to buy it.

You don't need to produce it.

You don't need to go anywhere.

You don't need to work for it.

Just let whatever occurs. Whatever comes up in your mind be, that is enough.

❋ ❋ ❋ ❋ ❋

Your mind has existed in you since the beginning. It is not something you lose or find. It is not something that exists or does not exist. This mind that you've had since the beginning thinks when you think, does not think when you don't think. This itself is the mind.

Whatever the mind itself thinks, whatever comes up, keep that in a relaxed and even manner, without trying to fix it, that is enough.

Then meditation becomes pleasurable and easy.

If it seems that spiritual practice is difficult, this is an indication that you are obstructed by your own negative actions. Some meditators do not let their necessary thoughts be as they are. With unnecessary deliberations they look far away, or grope at what is close by. If you do this, you won't understand the mind. You won't achieve it. You won't understand its significance. This is a challenge.

There is no reason for you to search far away or grope at what is near. Let that which searches far and gropes near be just as it is. That is it.

Some meditators do not let their thoughts just be when they are either thinking or not thinking. They think that success comes from doing the opposite. So they search far and grope at what is near. You will not recognize and realize the mind by searching far and groping nearby. There is no reason to search far and grope nearby.

If your mind is thinking, let it think. If your mind is not thinking, just let it not think. That is it.

❈ ❈ ❈ ❈ ❈

Some meditators are not sure if their mind is characterized by emptiness. They doubt this, wondering, "Is it empty? Is it not empty?" The problem is that they do not understand the significance of emptiness.

There is no need for doubt. Your mind has been empty from the beginning. Let it be in that empty state. That is it.

If you have doubt, let that doubt be just as it is. That is it.

Some meditators do not look at that which is doing the thinking, the mind. They look a great deal at the objects of their thinking, at their belongings, or at the ground, or at rocks. This is not the correct viewpoint. This is a dualistic viewpoint. Let that which thinks be just as it is, and then look.

Some meditators do not take the mind and that which appears to the mind to be inextricable. They chase the appearance. This is not the correct viewpoint, for in this viewpoint there are dualistic appearances. Don't chase the appearance over there, and don't fixate on the mind being a real object right here. Let that which appears and the mind be inextricable.

Some meditators do not let their mind rest in its own place. Like a cat waiting for a mouse, they look at whatever ideas occur. This is not the correct viewpoint. This is just expecting the thought. No matter whether ideas occur or don't occur, just let them be.

Some meditators do not know how to let the mind rest in itself. They see the last thought they had and follow it. This is not the correct viewpoint. This is just pursuing a thought. Let that which pursues the thought be, just as it is.

Some meditators do not let their mind rest wherever it is or wherever it goes. They crave perfect meditation, so they try to get up close to the mind to stare at it piercingly. This is not the correct viewpoint. Do not try to fix your mind. Do not attempt to work on your mind at all. Let it be where it is, whatever comes up, wherever it shines.

Some meditators repress whatever they think. They force it away and try to grab hold of the mind. This is not the correct viewpoint. It is suppression of thought. If the mind is stationary, let it be. If it is roaming, let it roam.

Some meditators keep their thoughts blank as they are ignoring them. This is not the correct viewpoint. This is just oblivion. Let your mind be clear and vivid in its empty state.

Some meditators just think that this blank thought is the mind itself and it is empty, and they cultivate this. This is not the correct view. This is a pseudo-emptiness. Let that which thinks this is emptiness be, just as it is.

Some meditators look at their thoughts when they are at ease, open, or feeling clear, but do not look at their thoughts when they are not at ease. This is not the correct viewpoint. This is accepting some states and rejecting others. Without accepting or rejecting anything, let whatever arises be, just as it is.

Some meditators look at their mind only when they have positive thoughts. They do not look when they have negative thoughts. This is not the correct viewpoint. This is simply looking for the good and ignoring the bad. Without looking for the positive thoughts or ignoring negative thoughts, let whatever thoughts arise be, just as they are, without wavering from them.

Some meditators are happy when they have a pleasing thought. But if wild ideas come up, they are angry at their own mind. This is not the correct viewpoint. The problem here is not knowing how to cultivate the essence of whatever thoughts arise. When wild thoughts come up, let those wild thoughts be in a relaxed state of mind, just as they are.

Some meditators focus or relax their thoughts when not needed. This is not the correct viewpoint. This is engaging in slightly too much correction. The problem is not knowing how to settle the mind. Apply focus or relaxation when necessary and avoid when unnecessary. Let your thoughts come as they will, clear and vivid.

Some meditators are not able to meditate when they recall the taste of delicious food or drink. Getting up, they think, "Perhaps I'll get something good to eat. Or maybe something good to drink." Then they go get something tasty to eat or drink. Acting in this manner will consume the nourishment of concentration, so your meditation will not be good. Delight in good food will make for the poorer concentration. So do not crave the taste of delicious food and drink, for you must consume of the nourishment of concentration.

Some meditators who are content and satiated with great wealth cannot meditate because they are too exuberant. When they encounter difficult circumstances, are ill, or are subject to criticism, they are also not able to meditate. Their faces become cloudy, their mouths spout complaints, and tears fall from their eyes. If you act like this, you will not gain skill in leveling your experience of pleasure and pain. Overwhelmed by the power of the eight mundane reactions to pleasure and pain, you will simply become a bitter practitioner. So it is important to level out your experience of pleasure and pain.

A Discussion of Freeing the Mind

From the beginning mind has not been some "thing."
When you search for it, you won't see it; it is empty.
And yet it is not just empty; it is aware and clear.
It is inseparably aware and empty, like the sky.

If you set it somewhere, it won't stay. It moves unhindered.
But if you don't set it, it will come back to its own place.
Mind doesn't have legs or arms, yet it runs everywhere.
If you send it somewhere, it won't go, just returns to its
    own place.

Mind doesn't have eyes, yet it is aware of everything.
Yet the appearances it is aware of become empty.
You can't claim, "The mind's essence is this."
Yet even if such an essence doesn't exist, awareness
    occurs in many forms.

Mind is not an existing thing, for it is empty.
It also is not *not* an existing thing, for it is aware of
    appearances.
Appearances and emptiness synthesized radiate with light.
This empty luminousness is the spiritual body's own
    brilliance shining forth.

It is the five forms of wisdom expanding outward.
It is the pure being of reality being spontaneously
    accomplished.
It is the spiritual body and the enlightened form of life
    shining forth without obstruction.
It is the mother of light coalescing with the child of light.

The real nature of the mind—
Do you understand it, learned people?
Do you know it, meditators?
Take it into your experience, practitioners!

An Instruction on the Self-Liberation of Confusion, which Turns Toxin into Remedy

In emptiness there is no greed.
Greed grows under the influence of confusion.
Look without confusion at that through which greed grows.
Look, cultivate that vision without distraction.

The greed will dissipate and become empty.
Rest without distraction in that empty state.
That is the purification of greed.
There is no greater gift than this.

How astounding is the practitioner who understands this.

❋ ❋ ❋ ❋ ❋

In emptiness there is no hatred.
Hatred grows under the influence of confusion.
Look without confusion at that through which hatred grows.
Look, cultivate that vision without distraction.

The hatred will dissipate and become empty.
Rest without distraction in that empty state.
That is the purification of hatred.
There is no greater discipline than this.
How astounding is the practitioner who understands this.

❋ ❋ ❋ ❋ ❋

In emptiness there is no anger.
Anger grows under the influence of confusion.
Look without confusion at that through which anger grows.
Look, cultivate that vision without distraction.

The anger will dissipate and become empty.
Rest without distraction in that empty state.
That is the purification of anger.
There is no greater patience than this.

How astounding is the practitioner who understands this.

❊ ❊ ❊ ❊ ❊

In emptiness there is no laziness.
Laziness grows under the influence of confusion.
Look without confusion at that through which laziness grows.
Look, cultivate that vision without distraction.

The laziness will dissipate and become empty.
Rest without distraction in that empty state.
That is the purification of laziness.
There is no greater diligence than this.

How astounding is the practitioner who understands this.

❊ ❊ ❊ ❊ ❊

In emptiness there is no distraction.
Distraction grows under the influence of confusion.
Look without confusion at that through which
    distraction grows.
Look, cultivate that vision without distraction.

The distraction will dissipate and become empty.
Rest without distraction in that empty state.
That is the purification of distraction.
There is no greater concentration than this.

How astounding is the practitioner who understands this.

❊ ❊ ❊ ❊ ❊

In emptiness there is no delusion.
Delusion grows under the influence of confusion.
Look without delusion at that through which distraction
    grows.
Look, cultivate that vision without distraction.

The delusion will dissipate and become empty.
Rest without distraction in that empty state.

That is the purification of delusion.
There is no greater wisdom than this.

How astounding is the practitioner who understands this.

❀ ❀ ❀ ❀ ❀

In emptiness there is no conceit.
Conceit grows under the influence of confusion.
Look without delusion at that through which conceit
    grows.
Look, cultivate that vision without distraction.

The conceit will dissipate and become empty.
Rest without distraction in that empty state.
That is the purification of conceit.
There is no greater gratification than this.

How astounding is the practitioner who understands this.

An Instruction on the Self-Liberation of Disturbing Emotions

If you transform your disturbing emotions into wisdom,
Suffering does not exist when you are focused.
Suffering emerges under the influence of confusion.
Look with focus at the nature of suffering.
Look, and cultivate that focus.

The suffering will cease to exist, will become empty.
Remain in that empty, clear state without distraction.
This is the purification of suffering.
This is known as the spiritual body of great happiness.

❀ ❀ ❀ ❀ ❀

Destructive emotions do not exist when you are focused.
Suffering emerges through the faults in your focus.

Look with focus at the nature of destructive emotions.
Look, and cultivate that focus.

The destructive emotions will cease to exist, will become empty.
Remain in that empty, clear state without distraction.
This is the purification of destructive emotions.
The spiritual body of no arising, this is called.

❋ ❋ ❋ ❋ ❋

Hatred does not exist when you are focused.
Hatred grows from faults in your focus.
Look with focus at the nature of hatred.
Look, and cultivate that focus.

Hatred will cease to exist, will become empty.
Remain in that empty, clear state without distraction.
This is the purification of hatred.
Mirror wisdom, this is called.

❋ ❋ ❋ ❋ ❋

Conceit does not exist when you are focused.
Conceit grows from faults in your focus.
Look with focus at the nature of conceit.
Look, and cultivate that focus.

Conceit will cease to exist, will become empty and clear.
Remain in that empty, clear state without distraction.
This is the purification of conceit.
Equalizing wisdom, this is called.

❋ ❋ ❋ ❋ ❋

Attachment does not exist when you are focused.
Attachment grows from faults in your focus.
Look with focus at the nature of attachment.
Look, and cultivate that focus.

Attachment will cease to exist, will become empty and clear.
Remain in that empty, clear state without distraction.

This is the purification of attachment.
Discriminating wisdom, this is called.

❀ ❀ ❀ ❀ ❀

Envy does not exist when you are focused.
Envy grows from faults in your focus.
Look with focus at the nature of envy.
Look, and cultivate that focus.

Envy will cease to exist, will become empty and clear.
Remain in that empty, clear state without distraction.
This is the purification of envy.
Active wisdom, this is called.

❀ ❀ ❀ ❀ ❀

Delusion does not exist when you are focused.
Delusion grows from faults in your focus.
Look with focus at the nature of delusion.
Look, and cultivate that focus.

Delusion will cease to exist, will become empty and
    clear.
Remain in that empty, clear state without distraction.
This is the purification of delusion.
The wisdom of reality's expanse, this is called.

❀ ❀ ❀ ❀ ❀

Torpor does not exist when you are focused.
Torpor gathers from faults in your focus.
Look with focus at the nature of torpor.
Look, and cultivate that focus.

Torpor will cease to exist, will become empty and
    clear.
Remain in that empty, clear state without distraction.
This is the purification of torpor.
Clear and empty wisdom, this is called.

✤ ✤ ✤ ✤ ✤

Anxiety does not exist when you are focused.
Anxiety grows from faults in your focus.
Look with focus at the nature of anxiety.
Look, and cultivate that focus.

Anxiety will cease to exist, will become empty and clear.
Remain in that empty, clear state without distraction.
This is the purification of anxiety.
Unchanging wisdom, this is called.

✤ ✤ ✤ ✤ ✤

The three poisons do not exist when you are focused.
The three poisons grow from faults in your focus.
Look with focus at the nature of the three poisons.
Look, and cultivate that focus.

The three poisons will cease to exist, will become empty
    and clear.
Remain in that empty, clear state without distraction.
This is the purification of the three poisons.
The three enlightened bodies' wisdom, this is called.

Remarks on Possible Experiences
When Working with the Mind

Here are a few remarks on possible experiences when working with the mind. Use these to develop confidence.

At times a meditator's mind may come to not think about
anything; it is just empty and vivid. In moments like this, do
not try to fix it. Just let it be vivid in and of itself.

At times your mind may come to be clear, vivid, and relaxed. In moments like this, let your mind be clear and vivid.

At times your mind may come to be dark, vague, vacant,
and unable to find clarity. In moments like this, employ clear
awareness, and let your mind be bare and awake.

At times your mind may come to be despondent. In moments like this, place yourself in a cheerful, relaxed, and joyful state.

At times your mind may settle for a moment or two, but not be able to settle for a long time, and there is murmur of thought going on. In moments like this, concentrate your surface thoughts while relaxing your inner thoughts.

At times your mind may be thinking or not. In moments like this, pull the mind up with vivid clarity, like pulling a hair out of butter, and set it in undistracted alertness.

At times your mind may be thinking of all sorts of things and is flopping up and down so much that it can't just be even for a moment. In moments like this, let your body relax. Let your mind relax. Do not lose yourself to distraction. Bring your mind around and settle it.

At times your heart may not be in your meditation, or you feel ill. In moments like this, offer earnest prayers to your spiritual teacher. Settle your mind in appearances of vibrant contentment and joy.

At times your mind feels ecstatic and bright. You have so much joy that you want to dance around! In moments like this, don't allow your mind to get too agitated. Place your mind in a state of shimmering relaxation.

Ascertaining the Basic State of Mind

The above things happen with the mind in cases where novice meditators have not ascertained the basic state of the mind. However, there is no reason for such things to occur to those who have ascertained it. Let me explain a bit why this is so.

> When you ascertain the basic state of the mind,
> You do not need to look attentively, for the mind's
>   luminosity naturally arises.
> You do not even need to meditate, for the mind keeps
>   itself in place.
> You will not be distracted, for the mind controls itself.
> You do not need to change a thing,

For this mindful awareness encompasses everything, just
   like the sky.

You do not need to fix anything,
For your mind is resting in a luminous state.
The spiritual body of your undistracted mind,
Is joined inseparably in luminosity,
With the spiritual body of a Buddha's mind.
It keeps itself in place without distraction,

And from emptiness, from the spiritual body itself,
Luminosity spontaneously emerges,
All while your own mind and the Buddha's mind are
   inseparable.
Spiritual bodies and pure states arise together.

You have neither hope nor fear. No selfishness. No
   pleasure or pain.
You are done with give-and-take. You are free of doubt.
This is what it is like when you have determined the
   nature of the mind.

Performing the Four Practices on
the Path of the Bodhisattva

When meditators move about,
They do not run around and jump about like madmen.
They move with body and mind at ease,
Their minds controlled and unwavering.

When meditators sit down,
They do not let their thoughts run on ceaselessly.
They straighten their posture,
And sit, with their mind set bare.

When meditators sleep,
They do not sleep in obscurity like a corpse.

They sleep the way a lion sleeps—
No distraction, in a state of brightness.

When meditators drink and eat,
They bless their food as if it were ambrosia,
As if their bodies were peaceful and wrathful deities.
They eat with undistracted minds.

Whether you are walking, sitting, or sleeping,
Be inseparable from emptiness,
Your mind inseparable from the Buddha's mind.
If you want to be without regret when you die,
You must practice contemplation in this way.

Working with a Qualified Teacher

You must know how to work with a qualified spiritual
     teacher.
You must be a renunciant, free of the world's turmoil.
You must be able to endure living alone in mountain
     retreat.
You must bear giving up love of food and clothing.
You must be diligent, never knowing a moment of
     distraction.
You must see without any dualistic appearances.
You must always meditate with focus and luminosity.
You must act without effort or choice.
Your goal must be for your mind to be inseparable from
     the Buddha's mind.
You must keep your vows with neither avarice nor
     artifice.
You must be free of longing for any object of desire.

Fortunate spiritual practitioners, practice these necessary
     meditations the best that you can.

Protection to Aid Your Meditation

If you want robust protection to aid your meditation,
   conduct yourself so:

Stop being a leader with many workers and followers.
Stop possessing so much wealth.
Stop keeping horses and livestock.
Do not become the head of a large family.

Stop being hostile toward rivals even as you are friendly
   to relatives.
Give up work, farming, or craft.
Quit laboring for wealth and reputation.
Stop seeking greatness, renown, and power.

If you do not cease these, distraction will carry your
   mind away.
If you stop this, your mind will become stable.
If your mind becomes stable, you will become a
   Buddha.

These days there are expert instructors and meditating
   students.
Many people benefit from understanding their own
   minds.
Many people benefit from understanding this point of
   true significance.

The fundamental nature of the mind—empty clarity—
Can dawn upon one and all.
Just ask people who understand this, and it will become
   clear to you.
Ask a lot of teachers, and understanding will come.
Remove your doubts in this way.

Then, meditate.

Ask People Who Are Learned

I would also like to discuss another important point for
    meditators:

These days there are also teachers who instruct poorly,
And students who meditate poorly.
They may meditate for seventy or eighty years.
And yet . . .

Many will achieve little contemplative experience and
    realization.
Many will not understand anything of true significance.
Many will perceive what doesn't exist to exist.
Many will unknowingly meditate in foolish ways.
Many will exert themselves pointlessly.

Expert instructors and meditating students,
Do not be self-important; ask people who are learned
So you may know your mind up and down.
Don't just make it up yourself!

Work in this manner so you may resolve your doubts,
Without spinning your head in circles!

CHAPTER TEN

PLACES OF SOLITUDE

INTRODUCTION

Where should one meditate? While any location should, in principle, be suitable for contemplative practice, Tibetan tradition praises the natural seclusion to be found in the mountains and high valleys of the Himalayas. In this chapter we shift from instruction and advice on meditation itself to look at ideal places for meditation: the landscapes, environments, dwellings, the domestic and wild spaces that have traditionally been connected with meditation. In chapter 1, the poet-saint Shabkar waxed eloquent about the wonders of mountain retreat, those secluded highland oases of contemplative practice. The selection translated in this chapter presents a more formal approach to finding and fashioning the idyllic place for meditation. The famous *Chariot of Knowledge: A Commentary on the Comfort and Ease of Meditation* by Longchen Rabjam (1308–1364) is a comprehensive manual of ethics, meditation, and theory of mind that covers everything from the foundation practices we have read throughout this book to philosophical reflections on the nature of reality and illusion. In the following passage, Longchen Rabjam offers a brief yet full account of what to look for when assessing a good location for meditation retreat.

Longchen Rabjam was the foremost philosopher of Nyingma School, the same school that Shabkar, Shenpen Tayé, and Patrul belonged to. While the latter three writers lived and work largely in the high mountains of eastern Tibet, Longchenpa was born on the high plain of central Tibet,

spending many of his years above the tree line, in an environment that is often rocky, dry, and challenging to manage.
And yet Longchenpa spent time in retreat among the high
cliffs above the Brahmaputra River, nestled far above Samyé,
Tibet's first Buddhist monastery. He also spent some of his
most important years of contemplation not in Tibet, but in
the green forested valleys of Bhutan. His hermitage in the
Bumtang region of central Bhutan—now the site of a famous
monastery, Tharpaling, the "Island of Liberation"—sits upon
a forested ridge, looking south upon the verdant dells of
Bhutan's Buddhist cultural heartland. It is no wonder that
Longchenpa's survey of the right type of place for meditation
includes several distinct environments. What the perfect location will be depends upon what kind of meditation one is
intending to practice, as well as the types of places that are
available where one lives.

"The Seasons" introduces the importance of climate in relation to landscape and environment. As we have seen in
Shabkar's poems in chapter 1, seclusion is ideal, for it is inherently serene. (We will hear challenges to this perhaps
overly idealized vision of wilderness in the following chapter.) Here we encounter the pragmatic side of the meditation
tradition; each season affords a distinctive location and style
of meditation. The dedicated practitioner who has the means
to travel can relocate throughout the year to places—and
climates—that are conducive to particular meditation practices.
Summer is for glacial mountains. Fall is for forests. Winter
for the lowlands. Spring for jungle, islands, or—as ever—the
mountains. Every type of Himalayan landscape, from the
high plateaus of Tibet to the lush forests of Nepal, Bhutan,
and India are included here, each offering a particular benefit
to the contemplative life. Significantly, Longchenpa also con-
nects the outer environment as well as lodgings with one's interior experience of being: "Summer is the season of the fire
element. Internal and external elements are all hot. So both
keep your dwelling cool, and keep to cooling activities." In
later forms of meditation (beyond the scope of this book),
where practitioners work creatively with visions of bodily

energy flows, this connection between person and environment becomes crucial. Here it is enough for Longchenpa to affirm that environment affects our physical and emotional sense of well-being, and that this relationship can be utilized to enhance one's contemplative practice.

"Locations for Meditation," "Place and Person," and "Assessing a Place for Meditation" offer a brief how-to guide for identifying a good spot for meditation. A range of landscapes, including mountain peaks, snowy or rocky mountains, forests, and riverbanks, are best suited for particular types of meditation. Yet wilderness is not the only place where meditation practice can flourish. Urban settings may be initially distracting for beginning meditators, but they may be perfect challenges for those who have developed skill in calm and insight meditation, whose "practice is firm." Be aware, also, of places that look good on the surface, but that may feature less obvious interruptions. Longchenpa speaks of serpent and earth deities that, from a Tibetan perspective, inhabit the landscape and can interact with the human realm in helpful as well as harmful ways. From a materialist point of view, one might mention, for instance, insects and other flora or fauna that inhibit meditation. There may be no greater deterrent to meditating on that bucolic lakeshore than a swarm of summer mosquitoes! By contrast, places that at first seem uninviting or scary may turn out to be, if one stays with it, particularly powerful places to meditate (Shabkar will speak about fears and dangers in wilderness locations in the following chapter).

"Different Uses of Meditation Locations," "Building a Dwelling for Meditation," and "Choosing a Good Place to Meditate" feature the built environment in addition to landscape. Some types of meditation, such as the "dark retreat," which is undertaken in total darkness, require purpose-built dwellings. Other activities, such as calm meditation, benefit from spaces that are marked out with gardens, fences, light interior spaces, and vistas. The larger point here is that an ideal place for meditation can be made even when it cannot be found. In this sense, Longchenpa provides guidelines for fashioning a contemplative space wherever one finds oneself. This is important today, with so many humans living in cities. Yet it was also important in Tibet's past. Longchenpa may have been able to find complete seclusion, but even he lived and worked among groups of people in monasteries, temples, and towns throughout his life. Patrul gave teachings to large audiences of laypeople who would have spent their days working among families and villages. And the Dalai Lama gave the meditation instructions that we read in chapter 2 to thousands of monks at a time, crammed into the city-like monasteries of Lhasa.

In the end, the perfect place for meditation is created through a combination of careful attention to the benefits and costs of wherever one finds oneself. Longchenpa encourages his readers to adopt not only a place-based approach to developing a successful contemplative practice, but a contemplative approach to environment, to the places we find ourselves in throughout our lives.

"WHERE TO MEDITATE," FROM *CHARIOT OF KNOWLEDGE: A COMMENTARY ON THE COMFORT AND EASE OF MEDITATION,* BY LONGCHEN RABJAM

The primary topic here is the place where you should practice.

The Seasons

We begin with the passing of the seasons:

> First, you should meditate in a place
> That is secluded and is joyful to experience,
> That is conducive to the contemplative practice
> According to the season.

In summer you should meditate in a cane or grass hut,
Amid glacial regions and mountain peaks.
Your hut should be cool and in a cool location.

In fall you should meditate in secluded forests,
On mountainsides, or rugged cliffs,
In a hut or dwelling of moderate temperature.
Adjust your food, clothing, and behavior appropriately.

In winter you should meditate in forests, caves,
Or other such warm lowland places.
Adjust your food, clothing, and bedding fittingly.

In spring you can meditate in the mountains, a jungle, or
     on a small island.
Stay in a dwelling that is conformable based on the heat
     or cold.
Adjust your food, clothing, and behavior appropriately.

This accords with the teachings that the great master Garab Dorjé gave in his work, *Profound Accomplishments of Yoga during the Four Seasons*.

Summer is the season of the fire element. Internal and external elements are all hot. So both keep your dwelling cool, and keep to cooling activities.

Fall is the season of the wind element. Internal and external elements have evolved. So both keep your dwelling open, clean, and bright, and maintain your activities to suit.

Winter is the season of the water element. Internal and external elements are cool. So keep your dwelling warm and undertake activities that warm you up.

Spring is the season of the earth element. Internal and external elements are just about to develop. So it is important that your dwelling balances heat and cold, and that your behavior is also balanced. This is so because the cycle of dependent arising occurs both internally and externally. As the *Wheel of Time Tantra* states, "As it is outside, so is it inside."

Locations for Meditation

Now I will point out the different kinds of locations and what they are best for:

The internal and external cycles of dependent arising
Are one and the same.
So reside in a place that provides both
A pleasant experience and appealing solitude.

On mountain peaks, one's awareness is clear and
    expansive,
So they are places for clearing away depression,
And where you can excel at creative visualization
    meditations.

In snowy mountains, creative visualization meditations
Are bright and awareness clear.
This is the place for cultivating insight meditation,
Where there are few hindrances.

In the forest, conscious thought is settled, and
This gives rise to a settled mind.
This is the place for cultivating calm meditation,
Where harmony predominates.

Around rocky mountains,
A desolate feeling of impermanence predominates.
Calm and insight meditation
Integrate and become clearer and stronger.

Riverbanks concentrate one's attention.
They renew feelings of existential melancholy and
    renunciation.

Cremation grounds are very powerful.
Here spiritual achievements come quickly.
They are taught to be best

For either creative or completion visualization meditations.

In places such as these, the novice, the intermediate, and
the highly experienced contemplative practitioner alike
will develop an improvement in their respective views
and meditations, as long as they rely on the previously
discussed behavior and knowledge for retreat. For the
good qualities of these places will serve as companions
as practitioners develop on the spiritual path.

Place and Person

Now I will present locations so that they may be understood in
relation to the contemplative experience of a given individual:

In towns, marketplaces, abandoned houses, and lone trees,
Where people, spirits, or ghosts wander,
Novices are distracted and disturbed.
Yet these places are praised as the best companions to
those whose practice is firm.

Temples, stupas, and other places inhabited by
malevolent spirits
Upset the mind and give rise to hateful thoughts.
Caverns and other places inhabited by lustful spirits
Give rise to attachment, and both lethargy and agitation
grow immensely.

Lone trees and other such places that wrathful muses
inhabit,
And cliffs or mountain spurs that violent spirits and
dangerous goblins inhabit,
Upset the mind and create bad conditions and hindrances.

Places that outcasts, serpent deities, and earth deities
inhabit,
Such as the lakeshore, green meadows, the wood, or herb
forests,

Or other delightful places strewn with flowers,
May seem nice at first, but later can be a hindrance.

Among these, places that worldly gods and unruly spirits
  inhabit are places to practice only for those meditators
  who have stable contemplative experience. For novices
  they are unsuitable either for meditation or for long-
  term residence, so they should avoid them.

You should always stay in good places that are inhabited
  by mountain deities, serpent deities, spirits, or other
  nonhuman beings who favor virtuous activity. They
  establish favorable conditions and help to ensure that
  adverse conditions do not occur.

Assessing a Place for Meditation

How should you assess a place?

In short, some places or dwellings are pleasing at first.
Yet, once familiar they are displeasing,
And thus, offer little concrete spiritual advancement.

Places that are scary and displeasing at first,
Become pleasing through familiarity.
Their power can be great.
They offer quick spiritual advancement and have few
  hindrances.

Most places beyond this are in the middle; they hold
  neither help nor harm.

These are the main important points. Assess a place for
  half a month; by then you will certainly know the place.

Your mind changes on the basis of your environment.
And the virtues of your practice increase or decrease.

So assess your environment.
This is taught to be very important.

For as the *Stages of the Path for Secret Mantra* says, "The characteristics of a place either promote virtuous development or detract from it."

Different Uses of Meditation Locations

Now, let's briefly describe types of places:

According to the four distinct activities
(Of calming, expansion, commanding, and subjugating).

Among the four types of places and activities,
Calming places naturally steady one's thoughts.
Expansive places please the mind,
Endowing it with a sense of grandeur and splendor.
Powerful places captivate and engross one's thoughts.
Intense places dizzy the mind, producing a sense of
   vivid fear.

If we distinguish every type of place, the list is endless.
So, for present purposes, calming places are the best for
   meditation.
The others, I fear, would take too long to describe.

Each location within the environment is conducive to one of the four activities. In calming places, the mind comes along naturally, giving rise to a nonconceptual contemplative state. Expansive places are landscapes of great grandeur that captivate the mind with pleasure. Powerful places produce feelings of attachment in one's thoughts. Intense places cause one to revel in fear.

The dimensions of places can be round, square, semicircular, or triangular. The color of a place can be white, yellow, red, or dark green. Additionally, each of the four types can occur as one of the other four types, so in total there are sixteen types. Really, the divisions are endless, but this is enough. Here I am teaching about calming places that increase and stabilize contemplative states.

Building a Dwelling for Meditation

The components for building in such a place are as follows:

> A meditation hut in a calming place,
> Should be set out of the way
> In a pleasing solitary location.
> An open vista with a clear view is ideal.

> A meditation hut in an open vista with a clear view
>   provides few hindrances for contemplative
>   development.
> Daytime and nighttime practices are distinct, so there are
>   different places for them:

> Night yoga requires a dark circular dwelling,
> With an elevated dark room placed within the center of
>   that circular dwelling.
> Place the headrest north,
> Just as the Buddha's was when he entered Nirvana.

> Day yoga requires a sunny place,
> With a grand and clear views of open space,
> With snow, waterfalls, forests, or landscape, and wide-
>   open skies.
> The mind is clear and bright here,
> Though the temperature should be moderate.

When you are preparing for nighttime yoga, construct the circular dark hut as follows: Some claim that the hut should be round like the sun, but this is really not good for moving about or sitting in the hut. So build a double-walled hut with a center in the middle. Place openings in the east, south, and west walls of the inner room. The distance between the interior wall and outer wall should be one arm span and an arrow length on each side.

Place the door in the west wall. The door of the inner wall should look south. The door of the outer wall should look west. At the four directions place four windows on the four walls so that you have light at other times. This will also be necessary if you need to perform circumambulations or other tasks. They should be shut when you are seated and meditating inside.

Meditate facing the door to the north. The place for daytime meditation should be on the roof of the hut, under a south-facing half roof. Meditate with a magnificent clear vista and you will have the best clarity during meditation.

Now, construct a dwelling for common calm meditation as follows:

> When you practice calm meditation,
> The ideal place is a retreat house surrounded by a fence,
> A place for the mind to develop stability naturally.
> When you practice insight meditation, a bright and clear
>   vista is important.
> It should always be pleasant and just right for the season.

To one side of your retreat house there should be open and spacious yard in a courtyard enclosed by a waist-high fence. Here calm meditation will develop naturally. Place a small seat on an elevated spot in that yard so that you can see into the distance. Here your insight meditation will develop naturally.

Now I'll describe the landscapes where both calm and insight meditation can develop.

> Forested valleys and other such low and dark locations
> Are places for calm meditation.

Snowy lands and other high places are places for insight
   meditation.
It is very important that you are aware of the differences.

Wherever you live, wooded forests and mountain gulches
Are places that direct the mind inward,
So they are ideal for the purpose of calm meditation.

High places open up awareness wide and clear,
So they are good for insight meditation.
Become familiar with this.

Choosing a Good Place to Meditate

Now I will summarize the meditation places described here,
so that you know how to choose them.

Briefly, in these landscapes and retreat dwellings,
Feelings of renunciation and existential melancholy emerge.
Your attention is focused, and your contemplation grows.
Because of this, these are places where you engage in virtue.
They are like the Heart of Enlightenment, so stay in them.

There are also places through which virtues are diminished
And destructive emotions grow,
Where disruptive commotion overpowers you.
These are places for the demons of damaging behavior.
   Intelligent people avoid them.

Padmasambhava has spoken about such places.
Those who hope for liberation should take note.

The locations and the types of dwellings where virtuous
practice can thrive, and where faith and the distinctive feelings
of renunciation can develop, are like the Heart of Enlightenment where the Buddha became enlightened. You should stay
in such places.

There are also places where strife and destructive emotions

grow. Here disruption and commotion thrive. Know that these are demonic places that foster damaging behavior. You must avoid such places.

Master Padmasambhava says in his *Garland of the Fortress of Views*, "Place is so important for those who practice the dharma. You cannot find a better place than one where one can work on the virtues and on authentic contemplation. So it is taught that you should live in such places. Those places where strife and non-virtue increase are impediments upon the path to liberation, so make an effort to avoid them."

Concluding Prayer

In landscapes where there is natural calm,
Nurtured with pure water, with the good fortune of
    ascetic practice,
And leaving the disturbing commotion of this life,
May I meditate on reality with deep contemplation.

May I leave the confines of the city of samsara,
The source of every kind of suffering,
And find that place of calm, of liberation, of authentic
    enlightenment,
The blissful garden of Nirvana.

These days a person such as myself can be of no benefit
    to living beings.
So may I quit the repetitive existence of these bad times,
    this worldly facade,
The disturbing commotion of this life,
And open the four doors to a precious hidden land.

CHAPTER ELEVEN

THE TRIALS OF SOLITUDE

INTRODUCTION

This chapter presents a complete overview of mountain retreat in the form of an extended dialogue in verse between a
Buddhist teacher and his student. The author Shabkar, whom
we have already met in chapters 1 and 4, responds to detailed
and direct questions from a student on the verge of retreat. In
earlier chapters, Shabkar used the spiritual song to idealize
the mountain retreat as the best possible place to practice
meditation (chapter 1), or to weave a tapestry of images
drawn from the natural world with the themes of impermanence and existential sorrow. In this, the last time we will
hear from Shabkar, he offers a very different message. Here
he brings the mountain retreat down to earth. Or, rather, the
voice of his student, Tubten Gyatso, does so. Tubten Gyatso
poses a series of twenty questions to Shabkar on the reasons,
experiences, and especially the challenges of life in mountain
retreat. The resulting dialogue is among the most vividly re-
alistic portrayals of the real-world difficulties that a meditator who is considering a sustained period of practice in
wilderness solitude may be faced with. When you step back a
bit, the dialogue can also be read as an exploration of the apprehensions that might arise for anyone preparing for contemplative practice.

This dialogue is remarkable for its candor about the many
things that can go wrong when one undertakes a meditation retreat that casts off the safety net of home, town, and social support. Ultimately, Shabkar is an optimist. Like his spiritual

successor Patrul, he offers lively and humane meditations on the inherently positive potential of the human mind. Yes, meditation may be challenging. And yes, the potential benefits of natural landscapes of solitude for meditation may need to be weighed against potential danger, hardship, and simple logistical challenges. But in the end, Shabkar encourages, the innate capacity of the mind to train itself is sufficient for the practitioner to succeed, to overcome obstacles and reap the rewards of meditation in mountain retreat.

In the final chapter, we will hear from Shabkar's most important predecessor in the tradition of Buddhist poet-saints, Milarepa, on the joys of meditation. But before we get there, we need to look at the difficulties that any meditator might encounter when they head "to the mountain."

The dialogues between Shabkar and Tubten Gyatso provide a sense of immediacy and intimacy. It is as if the disciple is directly questioning the master. Still, the *Golden Rosary of Mountain Spirituality* is a well-crafted, well-organized work of literature that covers a full range of contemplative topics and does so with the grace of song. The twenty topics include basic how-to advice on topics such as how to begin a contemplative retreat, the need for meditation in addition to learning and intellectual work, the best kinds of places to stay in retreat, the importance of separating oneself from the activity of home and town, and what food and supplies to bring to retreat.

The songs also venture into the psychological and emotional side of living apart from others. Here Tubten Gyatso expresses concerns that anyone considering solitary retreat might ask before committing to the practice. What should I do if bad things happen? What if I become lonely and depressed? What if I am afraid at night? Will the natural (or supernatural) world bring me harm? Who will teach me when I am alone? What if I run out of money and supplies? Or become ill? Shabkar answers each of these with confidence. And while each response to Tubten Gyatso's queries is unique, a general message of inspiration runs throughout the answers to these questions; the practitioner possesses greater powers of self-reliance than they might at first feel.

The mind is a powerful ally. It is resourceful and resilient. More than that, a mind that has already undergone training through meditation is especially flexible. A well-trained mind, assures Shabkar, is irrepressible, even in the face of emotional, physical, and environmental hardship.

Other songs address potential criticism of the very idea of heading off into the wilderness to meditate when a place at home or in town would be sufficient, or when it seems that there is so much that needs to be accomplished in the social world that is of more direct benefit than solitary retreat. These are powerful moments in this work, for they show the tradition interrogating itself, asking on the one hand if meditation is in fact a common good that is without any negative consequences, and on the other hand asking why anyone would leave the retreat if it were so good for meditation and the higher experiences said to come from meditation. Why, Tubten Gyatso is brave enough to ask, did the Buddha even return from the wilderness after his enlightenment? Shouldn't he have just remained there if the wilderness meditation retreat is all the wonderful things it is said to be? And why aren't there more people in retreat these days if it is so great? Questions of ethics also arise; as a religious specialist, Tubten Gyatso would have received invitations from laypeople in his community to perform rituals, to give blessings, to teach. Should he, a Buddhist leader, refuse these earnest requests? And aren't I, as the solitary retreatant, simply increasing my own renown, my own sense of importance, by separating myself from the rest of society?

These questions do not have easy answers. Shabkar responds to them in kind, assuring his disciple that the personal and social cost that meditation retreat seems to entail is illusory; crucial personal development is best carried out in the controlled environment of the meditation retreat, and this in turn has immense benefits for one's community, one's society. This is a classic Buddhist response to the question of meditation's utility for the social world in which most of us live. Yet the very fact that the *Golden Rosary of Mountain Spirituality* raises these questions illustrates how Buddhist tradition cross-examines its own fundamental practices. Every contemplative practitioner should also, the *Golden Rosary* suggests, think critically about the reasons, the scope, and the benefits of their contemplative practice.

We are not surprised that in the end Shabkar argues strongly for the value of meditation retreat, and for the value of wild places to the work of meditation. He spent most of his adult life traveling along the periphery of Tibet, living, working, and teaching in wilderness retreats throughout the high Himalayas. Yet mountain retreat is not the only way to develop contemplative skill. Remember, the Thirteenth Dalai Lama gave his instructions (chapter 2) to thousands of monks in the bustling city of Lhasa. The pragmatic orientation of the tradition assures that any place can be made into a place of retreat, as long as the practitioner can put their bit of "kusha grass" down and get to work. Symbolically, at least, the mountain retreat is the preeminent place of meditation in Tibetan tradition. Shabkar's advocacy for meditation in wilderness retreat affirms the importance of such places for contemplative work in Tibetan Buddhism.

In the final chapter, we will hear more about the joys of mountain retreat from Milarepa. Now let us sit in as the student Tubten Gyatso asks his teacher twenty insightful questions about the nature of solitary meditation.

A Golden Rosary of Mountain Spirituality

On this fair peak on Lakeheart Island,
Incense and pleasant fragrance billows.
Green trees flourish with ten thousand leaves.
Flowers shine brilliant colors.
Bees take up mournful song.

A sea swirls all around us.
Fish shimmer as they search for food.

Waves lap and move.
Waterfowl utter cries.

Above, upon the land of sky,
Clear moon and sun draw trails of light.
Gentle spring raindrops drip.
Rainbows sketch out forms in light.

Such wonders are endless,
Naturally entrancing the mind in this rocky cave.
Where lazy me just falls asleep.

But one night as I refreshed myself,
My student Tubten Gyatso came to speak with me.

What Should a Person like Me Do?

Tubten Gyatso:

I am in need of spiritual guidance.
You have trained your mind well,
Through engagement with the three trainings
Of ethics, contemplation, and learning.

You've heard many teachings and have knowledge of
    sacred texts.
You've understood the significance of deep spiritual
    vision.
You've more virtues than us students.
Your words are wise, your compassion vast.

You work for the benefit of others.
You never tire of teaching again and again.
You embody these ten virtues of a spiritual mentor,
And are a defender of humanity in this wicked age.

Now, in the midst of this wicked age,
What should a person like me do?
Please have mercy, grant me counsel!

Shabkar:

Ema! Free of hatred and prejudice,
Able to choose wisely,
So earnest in spirituality,
Faith in spiritual teaching and teachers,
Your thoughts well focused,
So capable, my beloved son.

Since I was young, I couldn't remember the teachings.
Even when I really tried to recall the teachings,
Half my life was lost in idle talk.

Now I think I don't know how much longer I have
    to live.
I didn't stay in a philosophical college.
I didn't study exoteric and esoteric scripture.
I've not looked at very many texts.
I've just sat alone in the mountains,
With advice that my mentor gave to me.

Other than that, I don't have a hairsbreadth's talent.
So I should just lie down to nap in silence.
The ignorant are at their finest when they speak little!

Have Mercy and Grant Me Your Words

Tubten Gyatso:

Master, you trained long, and your karma is excellent.
You had faith in the good teachings even as a child.
So faithful and devoted, you studied genuinely,

Listening to deep spiritual teachings from your mentor.

You did not squander the great value of freedom and
    opportunity.
You contemplated impermanence and death without
    regret.
You renounced the toils of this life.
Yet you were not lazy or apathetic.

Just like the old spiritual masters,
You meditated, not encountering a soul,
In so many hermitages and sites of solitude.
Your wisdom sprang forth from realizations in
    meditation.

Now you know all spiritual advice,
The essential meaning of exoteric and esoteric
    instructions,
And the spiritual songs you heard in times past.

Blue smoke rising in the sky,
Is a sign that there is a fire.
Spring rain is the voice of the turquoise dragon.
Gold may be found in the ground,
But its light is only reflected in the sky.

Realized yogins mostly
Express themselves in songs of realization.

When rain falls on the green spring meadow,
Sweet fresh flowers bloom.
When one prays to a wishing jewel,
All of one's desires are fulfilled.

When the flock of waterfowl takes off,
They offer such a joyous call.
When one prays to the learned mentors,
They impart such astute and fitting instructions.

You are a superior being in this degenerate time.
I must be meeting you here because of a prayer long ago.
If I can't hear any words of spiritual advice,
It's as if I'd never met you at all!

Master, look upon me with compassion.
Have mercy and grant me your words.

Shabkar:

My son, through the force of long-cultivated merit,
This life of yours is long and without illness.
You are blessed with good family, a good body, ability,
Power, wealth, wisdom, and adeptness.
You possess a human life, full of freedom and
    advantage.
All your companions in dharma possess great spiritual
    vision.

Whatever I've said in the past,
Was devoid of the artfulness that delights scholars.
No, I speak like a child,
In words that won't upset their elders.
But I wonder if whatever a fool like me says,
Won't upset those learned intellectuals.

If you like what children and the elderly say,
If you like what the foolish say and want more,
I'll talk about whatever this yogin can recall.
Fortunate son, listen without distraction!

The best spiritual paths, deep and unerring,
That are well-known in snowy Tibet,
Are the Middle Way, the Great Perfection, the
    Great Seal,
Pacification, and Severance.
In each of these
You first learn and critically analyze the teachings,

And earnestly integrate them into your contemplative
    experience.
This is how you must meditate.

Do I Need to Meditate after Learning
and Critically Analyzing?

Tubten Gyatso:

I remember the sufferings of the three negative realms
    of life.
You who preserves from these,
My illustrious and precious mentor,
You who keep me well in refuge,
With the support of the Buddha, dharma, and sangha:

These days there are many who can learn and think.
Yet there are so few who can actually meditate!

Do I need to meditate after learning and critically
    analyzing?
Is it not enough just to have knowledge?

Shabkar:

Son, listen here with no distractions.
Milk is surely the source of butter.
But if it is not churned, it will not become butter.
Sesame is surely the source of oil.
But if it is not pressed, where will the oil come from?

After learning and analyzing, if you do not meditate,
You will not attain the result, enlightenment.
So knowledge is not enough;
You must meditate single-pointedly on your knowledge,
    this is vital.

Where Should I Stay for the Meditation to Be Good?

Tubten Gyatso:

You've understood cause and effect without error.
You've rejected sin and perfected virtue.
Relying on that, you've ascended the peak of bliss.

Distinguished, precious mentor,
Learning and analyzing not being enough,
I'll rely on single-pointed meditation.

Where should I stay for the meditation to be good?
Please show a fool like me.

Shabkar:

Listen well, faithful one.

The person who engages in meditation
Cuts the bonds of the eightfold everyday syndromes—
Gain, loss, fame, infamy, praise, blame, pleasure, sorrow.

Avoid places of hustle and bustle,
And, just as in the lives of the old masters,
You must go meditate in a hermitage.

What If I Do Not Avoid Places of Hustle and Bustle?

Tubten Gyatso:

You've seen the cycles of suffering, like the fiery depths of
    a hell realm.
You've protected the three trainings, in particular morality,

Like the apple of your eye.

Distinguished, precious mentor,
What if I do not avoid places of hustle and bustle?
Where is the fault in that? Please tell me.

Shabkar:

Listen now, my virtuous and diligent student.
Without living in solitude, it is hard to gain
     liberation
For people who delight in the hustle and bustle.

People who live amidst the hustle and bustle
Always engage the five negative emotions, the eightfold
     everyday syndromes,
The ten unvirtuous behaviors, and the five obstructions
     to concentration.

The ten virtuous behaviors,
The three trainings,
The six perfections,
The three vows,
The creation and completion forms of visual meditation,
The Great Perfection,
Practice in spiritual vision, meditation, and post-
     meditative conduct,
The ten spiritual practices,
Collecting merit and wisdom—
The world of hustle and bustle offers no path through
     these.

Where is there calm meditation, insight meditation, or
     concentration in that world?

So the Buddha described on many occasions
The faults and defects of the world of hustle and bustle.

If the Buddha Had Stayed in Solitude

Tubten Gyatso:

After cultivating a wish to become enlightened,
The Buddha and his spiritual children practiced
The six perfections, the four methods for gathering
    disciples,
And other magnificent, good works.

But to do this they remained long in the world of hustle
    and bustle.
If they had stayed in solitude, what would the value have
    been?

Shabkar:

You who are generous and free of attachment, listen.

If you renounce life in the hustle and bustle,
And go to live like an ascetic,
Alone, in the solitude of the mountainside,
The faults and defects will naturally disappear
    for you.

Through the power of solitude, you will attain every
    valuable quality.
Since you will be free of any attachment to belongings,
Through living in the hermitage, you will perfect the act
    of giving.

Free of any objects or conditions that give rise to
    attachment,
Your moral discipline will be pure.

You will not encounter horrendous conditions,
So will naturally be patient and not prone to anger.

By living alone, you will become possessed of
   diligence.
With no hustle and bustle around, your meditation will
   increase.

You won't have anything else to think about than
   spiritual teachings,
So wisdom will be born in you,
And you will naturally develop both mindfulness and
   introspection.

The ten virtuous actions, the three trainings,
The three vows, creation and completion modes of visual
   meditation, Great Perfection,
Practice in spiritual vision, meditation, and post-
   meditative conduct, the ten spiritual practices,
Collecting merit and wisdom: all of these will naturally
   increase.

Calm meditation, insight meditation, and concentration
   will grow on their own.
You will attain every spiritual capacity, from mundane to
   supreme.

Because of this the Buddha and his spiritual children
Have spoken many times of the virtues of solitude.

Won't Adverse Circumstances Arise?

Tubten Gyatso:

Your calm meditation is complete, you've stopped
The conceptual winds and kindled the flame of insight
   meditation.
You see the nature of reality like I see a painting!

Illustrious, precious master,
When I am living in solitude at the hermitage,
Won't adverse circumstances arise?

Shabkar:

You have learned a lot but listen again now.
You will be living at a hermitage.
There is no boss in an empty valley, amidst mountains
    and cliffs!

The birds and the wild animals who live there
Won't utter a single unpleasant word.

There is no reason to bring any wealth or goods with
    you,
So you have no need to fear bandits or thieves.

There will be no objects that give rise to attachment or
    hatred,
Discord and adverse circumstances are naturally absent.

What Provisions and Gear Would Be Best to Bring?

Tubten Gyatso:

You received empowerments and preserved your sacred
    commitments.
Creation and completion and Great Perfection you've
    integrated into your experience.
You've actually achieved realization on the good spiritual
    path.

Illustrious and precious mentor,
When I stay in the hermitage,
What provisions and gear would be best to bring?

Shabkar:

Modest son, listen again now.

Your perfect provisions and gear are already complete:
Earth cave, rock cave, a hanging rock,
These fine unconstructed houses are a joy to experience.

Cascading streams and animals,
Sweet-smelling plants and forests,
And many flowers to make healing incense.
Greens and fruit trees,
And many tasty things to eat.

When you need something, you must do it yourself,
But there is no one else around to be greedy about it!

The hunter, the shepherd, the wood collector,
Has faith in the virtuous ascetic living in a hermitage,
So they procure your provisions and gear.
When they go to the village, they say good things
   about you,
And through this the faithful men and women in the
   village
Provide what food, clothing, and gear they can.

So you should make the journey to the hermitage!

Why Are So Few People Staying on the Mountain Today?

Tubten Gyatso:

You are learned in all the profound textual traditions.
You are disciplined, unsullied by transgression of vow or
   moral blemish.

You benefit others through your aspiration to
   enlightenment.

Illustrious and precious mentor,
So there is nothing harmful, no adverse circumstances,
   and no obstacles,
While one is alone at the hermitage,
So one's provisions are made complete, and there are
   spiritual practitioners around,
So it is right that all should go into retreat.

Yet there are so few people staying on the mountain today.
What is the reason for this?

Shabkar:

Conscientious one, listen again now.

A hermitage where there is nothing harmful,
No adverse circumstances, and no obstacles,
Where one's provisions are made complete,
And there are spiritual practitioners around,
Such a place of solitary hermitage
Is greater than even the wondrous realm of the gods.

The unfortunate do not recognize it.
Those who think too much develop doubts about it.
Those who have merit within the world of hustle and
   bustle
Put it off, lose the opportunity, and their good fortune
   runs out.
So there are few people staying on the mountain.

These paradises that are solitary hermitages
Are the byways of long-gone saints.
They are where the holy ones of today remain.
They are where future fortunate ones will go.
They are where the learned and righteous aspire to be.

Do You Become Depressed Being Alone?

Tubten Gyatso:

You have achieved the highest learning and realization,
Yet you distance yourself from your followers and their
   wealth,
Keeping only to the acts of a mendicant.

Illustrious precious mentor,
When you are living for a long time at the hermitage,
Alone, with no companions,
Do you not become depressed during the days?

Shabkar:

You wise one, listen again now.

On the slopes of the glorious mountain,
If you want company, well, there are many joyous
   friends:
Wild animals of many shapes and colors
Wander carefree and beautiful.
They play together and call out to each other.
After a while they get used to you and walk right up.

In the rains of spring and summer,
The flowing rivers are turquoise.
Under trees with flowers and fruit,
Thousands of songbirds merrily fly,
Every stream calls out sounds as they fall.
They quench the pangs of thirst for all who drink.

The valley meadows are brilliant with flowers.
Swarms of bees circle, singing their songs.

On green plains and rivers across the empty valleys,
Shepherds care for their horses and cattle.

By the shores of lakes and ponds,
Geese with fair cries delightfully glide.

All day long, there is no chance to be depressed.
The labor and toil of the hustle-bustle world is absent here.

If one associates with people, antagonism will arise.
So it is good be alone, out on your own.

Are You Afraid at Night?

Tubten Gyatso:

You are alone like a lion,
Staying always in solitary hermitage.

Living without fear, you work for spiritual ends.
Yet even though you are not sad during the day,
Are you not fearful at night?

Shabkar:

Gentle and open-minded one, listen again now.

The yogin who understands that the self does not
    ultimately exist
Has no fear of the night.

But if they have a moment of fear or alarm in retreat,
Using this fear to see things correctly,
They recall their mentor who incited them to virtue.
They never forget, and always get back to meditation.
They quickly achieve presence of mind.

In the city the hustle and bustle distract you by day.
And by night you are careless in your sleep.

There is never a chance to achieve presence of
  mind.

It is vital that even-minded yogins
Meditate in a place that keeps you alert.

Can You Be Harmed by Inhuman Forces?

Tubten Gyatso:

Clouds of kindness and compassion gather,
A dharma rain falls upon living beings,
So that the harvest of harmony is bountiful.
You know this, illustrious and precious mentor.
Yet when you are in solitary hermitage,
Couldn't you be harmed by inhuman forces?

Shabkar:

Thoughtful child, listen again now.

When you meditate upon the vision of selflessness,
Elemental demons, inhumans, and other beings whose
  thoughts are toxic,
Well, their toxic minds are pacified,
And they begin to aspire to enlightenment!
You don't need any other armor than meditation.

Living in solitary hermitage,
You are favored and blessed
By your mentor, the gods, and the spiritual muses.
Buddhas and bodhisattvas everywhere
Consider you to be their child, and always watch
  over you.
The gods who delight in spiritual teachings
Always clear away any obstacles for you.

In Retreat Who Will Teach Contemplative Instructions to Me?

Tubten Gyatso:

With a demeanor cultivated through learning,
    consideration, and meditation,
You always behave without malice
Toward friends, patrons, and householders.

Illustrious and precious mentor,
Yet when I am in solitary hermitage,
Who will teach contemplative instructions to me?

Shabkar:

Kindhearted one, listen again now.

When you live in solitary hermitage,
There are many who know how to teach contemplation.

With the changing of the four seasons,
The colors of the plants and trees change.
New flowers transform into old.
Hoarfrost emaciates the vegetables and crops.
The wind turns the grain into broken bits.

Birds in the groves gather, then scatter.
Falling rains intensify, then recede.
Lakes and ponds freeze, then melt.
Waterfowl flock together, then fly apart.
Wild animals move about impulsively.

The sun, moon, and stars rise, then set.
The years, the months, the days pass by.

Every single animal and plant speaks,
"The stuff of samsara has no permanence to them at all!"

Again and again they symbolically illustrate
   impermanence.
And in this condition, they experience sorrow.

Birds care for the chicks,
Wild animals defend their young.
By this they say, "You must be kind to living
   beings!"
By this they symbolically illustrate kindness and
   compassion.

Based upon this you can cultivate
Kindness, compassion, and the aspiration to
   enlightenment,
Within your own mind in an authentic way.

The clear autumn sky symbolically illustrates
The empty yet luminous awareness that is the body of
   reality,
Saying, "I am like that!"

Based upon this the hermit
Comes to understand the meaning of the unborn body of
   reality.

Rainbows shining in the sky,
Fog encircling the middle of the snowy mountain,
The mirage that moves upon the plain,
These all say, "The phenomena of all reality are
   like that!"
They symbolically illustrate that everything lacks
   absolute existence. It is all empty.

Based upon this you come to understand
That all things are empty, lacking absolute existence.

If you know this, the material world becomes
A master who teaches sacred spiritual lessons.

If You Become Impoverished, What Should You Do?

Tubten Gyatso:

Mindful person carrying the pacifying weapons,
You are the foe of desire and other toxic emotions,
As soon as they arise, you defeat them.

Illustrious and precious mentor,
When staying in solitary hermitage,
If you become impoverished, what should you do?

Shabkar:

Compassionate one, listen again now.

Living without desires in the hermitage,
Your nourishment is prepared by the nonhuman muses.

For the yogin who is free of all hatred and desire,
Everything you might desire is in fact reality itself.

If you should become impoverished,
Ideally you would eat concentration for your meal!

More moderately, eat extracts from green vegetables.
Or at least you can go begging for alms,
Collect just a bit, then hurry back to the hermitage.

Do not covet the taste of those alms or patrons' praise.
For if you covet alms and praise,
The taste of your spiritual experience will become spoiled,
And faults and defects are all that will come to you.

So, my faithful, beloved son,
Like wind in the sky, don't covet anything,
Like a wild animal, live in solitary retreat.

If you've amassed great riches,
Do not become bloated with pride.
And if you are poor, do not lose heart!

What Do I Do If I Become Ill?

Tubten Gyatso:

Others steal your wealth,
You even allow them to steal from you.
You give it away! Because you are happy,
You do not covet those things.

Distinguished, precious mentor,
When living in solitary retreat,
What do I do if I become ill?

Shabkar:

You with your thoughts set upon enlightenment, listen
   again now.

When suffering or illness of any kind
Befalls the person living in the hermitage,
They need not search for any means,
No medicine, no therapy,
Other than meditation
Upon the mentor's instructions, or
On the aspiration and cultivation of enlightenment.

Throughout the big events and the small in this life,
Quit cherishing your own physical existence.
Transform the five mental and physical materials into
   nourishment.
The events of life will calm down on their own.

Even if you contract a severe illness,
And it is certain you will die,
If you die in service of spiritual practice,
   very good!
Your place of death will be the retreat.

Don't descend to the village,
Thinking to get just one dose of medicine.
Like a wounded wild animal,
Your death will not be heard by anyone.
Your rotten corpse will not be seen by birds.
This is the way to die in retreat.

Are You Serving the Needs of Others at All?

Tubten Gyatso:

As if they have done no harm to you,
Were someone to cut off your head,
You would bear no anger toward them.

Distinguished, precious mentor,
Living continuously in solitary retreat,
Are you serving the needs of others at all?

Shabkar:

Inquisitive one, listen again now.

Like a wounded animal,
Living alone in solitary retreat,
You naturally serve the needs of others.

Living in the hustle and bustle,
Giving dharma talks around town,
You won't be of much benefit to people.

In today's decadent world,
When people arrive to meet you,
Run away and hide.
If you meet them on the path, walk away quickly,
For if you talk for very long it is so easy to gossip.

They won't give gifts to those in need of food and
     wealth,
While they pile presents up in front of those who need
     nothing.
When scholars give teachings, they don't listen
While they beg for teachings from the
     uninformed.

So apart from civilizing backward people,
Stay in solitary hermitage,
Working hard on your spiritual development.

Even the cheats, the wild men, the sinful
Will experience intense faith and zeal down deep,
When they see you living in solitary retreat.

So, my son, for the sake of others,
Always maintain your solitary retreat.

Should I Refuse Invitations from the Faithful?

Tubten Gyatso:

Your burden is heavy, yet you give to others,
Never swelling with pride. Peaceful,
You are charming to everyone.

Distinguished, precious mentor,
If faithful people come to invite me,

Should I refuse to go with them?

Shabkar:

My eloquent son, listen again now.

If faithful people invite you to town,
Use foresight; if the time has come
For them to be trained, then go.

If the time is wrong, then think of this
As a demon's deception; no matter how high
    they are,
Don't leave your solitary retreat.

If you can go a single time,
They will need you to go
Many, many times after that.
Then ever after the demon will carry you
    down
Through the mountains to the valleys.

When you become stable in your solitude,
Test the stability of your meditative experience and
    realization
By considering this:

Beyond a bit of grasping or wandering,
If your mind becomes free of desire on its own,
Your initial meditative experience should be
    good.

Then until you attain enlightenment,
Carry your mentor as your highest concern.
Hold on to solitary retreat like you hold on to
    your hat,
Herd the enlightened attitudes like you do your cattle.

Defend your vows and commitments as you do the apple
  of your eye.
Cast out pride and conceit as you would poison.

What Harm Will Come from Conceit and Pride?

Tubten Gyatso:

When even people you protect like children,
Act like enemies toward you,
You redouble your immense kindness toward them.

Distinguished, precious mentor,
If I cultivate conceit and pride,
What harm will come about?

Shabkar:

Mountain son, listen again now.

People in solitary retreat experience conceit,
Pridefully thinking, "I am so good!"
They praise themselves and disparage others.
This is the demon deluding you, making you conceited.

Pride and conceit are obstacles on the path to
  enlightenment.
By disparaging others, you cast yourself into destructive
  states of life;
It will be an eon until you reach enlightenment, even
  staying in retreat!

This is an undeniable reason,
So do not engage in pride and conceit.
Do not praise yourself or disparage others.

How Should We Engage in Contemplative Experience?

Tubten Gyatso:

You are free of all faults,
And full of all good qualities.
Unique refuge for people in this degenerate era,

Distinguished, precious mentor,
When in the solitude of retreat,
How should we engage in contemplative experience?

Shabkar:

Resilient one, listen again now.

When you are staying in solitary retreat,
Wear whatever ragged clothes you have,
Eat what food there is, appetizing or not.
Drink what there is, salt and spice or not.

Never be seen by people,
For if people see you at all, it will be
Just like the time people saw Reverend Milarepa,
Living on nettle soup,
Starving, emaciated, with dark complexion, and said,
"How pitiful this person is!"
Tears fell from his bitter enemies.

"Now I will take up the practice!"
Make this sincere oath three times.
Keep what is truly valuable in your heart.
Reflect continuously on the unpredictable certainty of
    death.

"I have come to this solitary hermitage.
If, without integrating this into my experience,

I come to desire people, wealth, and sustenance,
Where will these come from if not the world?
But I must not deceive myself!
For I might think, 'If I've integrated the sacred spiritual
    teachings
Into my experience, what need is there to
Give up the world for this solitary retreat?'
But I won't stay in the ordinary world, I'll cultivate
    resilience,
Until I've developed exception experience and realization,
Even if my bottom rots, even if my cushion bursts, even if
    I die, it's all worth it."

Reflect in this way, give up the world, and
Integrate your mentor's instructions into your experience.

What Will Happen When I Integrate the Instructions into My Experience?

Tubten Gyatso:

Like a precious wishing gem,
Bestowing whatever one wishes,
Fulfilling whatever one wishes for,

Distinguished, precious mentor,
When I do integrate these instructions into my experience,
What will happen in the present? What will happen
    ultimately?

Shabkar:

Spiritual son, listen again now.

If you integrate these instructions into your experience,
Presently you will experience joy, happiness, and praise.

Ultimately you will be completely enlightened.

As long as there are still living beings in cyclic existence,
You will work for the good of every sentient being, no
   exceptions.

This golden rosary of fine mountain spirituality,
I, a yogin who loves the mountain,
Spoke while staying at Lakeheart Hill,
For you, my mountain-dwelling son.

Tsokdruk Rangdröl wrote these responses to the
   questions of his student Tubten Gyatso.

CHAPTER TWELVE

SHEER JOY

INTRODUCTION

We conclude the book with songs from *The Black Treasury: Life and Songs of Milarepa*, songs that express the sheer joy encountered in meditation retreat by centuries of Tibetan contemplative masters. Milarepa (circa 1040–1123) is the single-most important poet-saint of Tibet, as well as the most widely known and popular symbol of meditation in mountain retreat, of Buddhist contemplative life amid the snow peaks of Tibet. What the Buddha began on the plains of India millennia ago, Milarepa continues on the high slopes of the Himalayas. Milarepa also stands at the beginning of the traditions surveyed in this volume. While we have drawn from ten authors who flourished throughout a thousand-year period and five distinct schools of Tibetan Buddhism here, each would acknowledge the importance of Milarepa as a great writer on meditation and the contemplative life, but also as a central icon of the traditions of Tibetan Buddhist meditation as a whole. Milarepa closes the volume, but he brings us right back to where we began, to the opening scenes of Shabkar's songs in praise of heading "to the mountain," to the meditation seat, to the work of taming and refining the intense energy of one's own mind.

The seven songs translated here offer encouragement to anyone who has undertaken the practices described in the preceding chapters. Each song works to capture the simple, sheer joy that comes through meditation, both as an outcome of enhancing the capacity of the mind to focus on the immediacy of life, and through the very work of meditation itself, moment by moment, day by day, year by year. "Like a Prisoner Freed" offers twelve vivid similes with which to imagine the joy of the yogin—the contemplative practitioner—at different points in their career, from the moment they find contemplative solitude to that time, however distant, that they come to be "beyond rebirth," enlightened.

"Castle in the Sky" features one of Milarepa's famous retreat centers, White Rock Horse Tooth in southwest Tibet, just north of the Nepal border. This song pairs the mundane details of meditation—the meditation strap that holds one's knees firm during periods of long practice, the canopy of trees that lends shade in summer—with finer points of Buddhist philosophy—the illusory body that integrates the physical and trans-physical, or the natural luminosity of the mind, a topic we encountered in chapter 6 on insight meditation.

"Green Rocky Mountain" situates a brief praise of body, speech, and mind—a classic Buddhist triad connoting the entirety of one's being as it is enmeshed and enhanced within contemplative practice—in an ephemeral moment of meditation amongst the southern Tibetan wilderness. In "Mountain Clouds" Milarepa sings words of encouragement to his student Rechung as he ponders the value of solitary meditation, assuring him that "contemplatives whose meditations are their own [are happy] no matter where they go."

"Forest Mountain" is perhaps the most reminiscent of Shabkar's songs among the seven, praising the simple advantages of a life brought down to quiet fundamentals in retreat: "nothing to seek, nothing to attain, what sheer joy." "In This Forest Hermitage" personifies the mountain, bringing the landscape alive as it provides protection to the practitioner on all sides: "Mountain rocks like spiritual champions and muses; mountain face like a god's castle; mountain slope like a mother's lap; mountain right like a banner unfurled; mountain left like a lotus in bloom."

Finally, "Meditation Experience Flashes" shifts focus from

the exterior landscape to the interior contemplative environment, where the positive results of meditation illuminate
one's being, like flashes of lightning, or like a bird's wing suddenly catching the sunlight on its tips. Poetry here becomes a
contemplative tool to imagine a radically different kind of
thought, a radically different timbre of emotional resonance
than is so often experienced in daily life. Contemplative experience "flashes," illuminating life in unexpected moments,
infusing mind with powerful luminous energy and soaring
feelings of freedom. Meditation, Tibetan Buddhist poets of
contemplative life would have it, fills our days with nothing
more or less than joy.

THE BLACK TREASURY, BY MILAREPA

Like a Prisoner Freed

Like a prisoner freed from a pit,
The yogin who has given up homeland is joyful.

Like a fine horse untied from the straps,
The yogin who is freed from objectification is
    joyful.

Like a wild animal who won't live below,
The yogin who stays in solitude is joyful.

Like a vulture soaring the sky,
The yogin with sure philosophical vision is
    joyful.

Like the wind moving through the sky,
The yogin unobstructed is joyful.

Like a shepherd prospering with good sheep,
The yogin cultivating emptiness and clarity in
    contemplative experience is joyful.

Like Mount Tisé in the middle of it all,
The yogin unmoving, unchanging, is joyful.

Like the flow of a great river,
The yogin with unceasing contemplative experience is
    joyful.

Like a corpse in the cemetery,
The yogin who has abandoned work is joyful.

Like a rock cast into the sea,
The yogin who will never turn back is joyful.

Like the sun and moon shining in the sky,
The yogin in whom light shines everywhere is
    joyful.

Like a leaf cut from the palm tree,
The yogin beyond rebirth is joyful.

These twelve melodies of the joyful yogin,
You, yogin, must always carry this upon the spiritual
    path.

Castle in the Sky

White Rock Horse Tooth, castle in the sky,
To this high castle among sky castles,
I, Milarepa the Tibetan
Went to meditate in single-pointed concentration.

Above, the Nepalese trees make a canopy—joy.
Below, moss makes a cushion—joy.
This illusory body has just the right nourishment—joy.
Meditation strap circles me a single time—joy.

My mentor's instructions are in my thoughts—joy.
I understand the immaculate vision—joy.
I meditate united with luminosity—joy.
I practice effortless self-liberation—joy.

I keep my commitment without pause—joy.
The three spiritual bodies are the spontaneous result—
     joy.
And joy such as this,
Is joy in which misery is simply impossible!

Green Rocky Mountain

In this green rocky mountain castle,
Milarepa's meditation is joyful.

I live without attachment and craving—joy.
My illusory body is free of illness—joy.
I live with no despair—joy.

My contemplations know no famine—joy.
My inner heat knows no cold—joy.
My spiritual discipline is undaunted—joy.

My chores are not an ordeal—joy.
My solitude knows no distraction—joy.

Such is my body's bearing.

My spiritual path contains both means and wisdom—
     joy.
My contemplative experience contains both the creation
     and integration of deities—joy.
The vital energies of my consciousness are stable—joy.
I am silent, with no one I must speak to—joy.

Such is my speech's bearing.

My spiritual vision does not grasp at appearances—joy.
My meditation is uninterrupted—joy.
My conduct after meditation knows no fear—joy.
My successes transcend hope and fear—joy.

Such is my mind's bearing.

Unchanging, nonconceptual luminosity—joy.
In a space where truth and falsity are purified, I am
    joyful.
An expanse of unimpeded imagination, I am joyful.

This little melody of intense joy,
Puts my contemplative experience into song.
A bit of advice that slipped from mouth,
That unites vision and practice.

Future seekers of enlightenment,
If you want to experience this song's meaning, practice in
    this way!

Mountain Clouds

By my mentor's blessing I've gone into retreat.
Happy is the beggar's homeland, the mountain clouds.

There is not another soul, yet the gods keep me company.
Happy am I surrounded by benevolent gods.

This deserted valley, only the muses visit here.
Happy am I with muses' exalted sign language.

Happy I am, no interruptions to my good meditations.
How happy am I as experience and realization dawn.

I commune with good and righteous friends.
If your meditation is ardent, how happy are heart
and mind.

Good food is tasty when not given but earned.
How happy I am as I taste the best food, interior
contemplation.

Good meditation is supported by mindful
awareness.
Drink the drink of no distraction and be sated.

Contemplatives whose meditations are their own,
How happy they are no matter where they go.

Rechung, my son, cease your desire for common
happiness.
You've no time for impermanent things now, so armor
yourself,
Go now to meditate in the deserted valley.

Forest Mountain

In this power place, a secluded forest mountain,
What joy, such joy living in solitude.

There's no racket, what sheer joy.
A seat of moss beneath me, what a joy.

There are no people here, what sheer joy.
Alone in a canopy of Nepal trees, what a joy.

Nothing to seek, nothing to attain, what
sheer joy.
My interior warmth is blazing, what a joy.
Not hot, not cold, what sheer joy.

I don't speak, given it up, what a joy.
Nothing to say, no one to say it to, what sheer joy.

My breathing is neither coming nor going, what
    a joy.
Agitation has ceased, what sheer joy.

My mind is without fear, what a joy,
No drowsiness and distraction, what sheer joy.

Luminous contemplation dawns, what a joy.
Clarity without obscuration, what sheer joy.

I've no desire for wealth, what a joy,
No attachment, what sheer joy.

I've no craving for food, what a joy,
No hunger, what a sheer joy.

I've no family ties, what a joy,
I am without hatred, what sheer joy.

No hatred for enemies, what a joy.
In harmony with everything, what sheer joy.

My spiritual vision is non-dual, what a joy.
I don't grasp at the surface of things, what
    sheer joy.

My meditation is continuous, what a joy.
There is no "meditation" or "not meditation," what
    sheer joy.

My practice is without pretense, what a joy.
I don't accept this, reject that, what sheer joy.

There is no great or small path, what a joy.
I realize the unity of meaning, what a joy.

However I work with my mind, what a joy.
Nothing to seek, nothing to attain, what sheer joy.

And through this yogin's joy,
May every living being experience joy!

In This Forest Hermitage

Ema! In this forest hermitage,
This happy cave of white rock, the Sun Fortress,
In this fastness we know freedom of thought, what a joy!

In this retreat where contemplative experience is born,
We know lucid awareness, what a joy!

We don't need to go anywhere, the scenery a joy.
Firewood is abundant, an effortless joy.
Not a voice to hear, lust and hate vanished.

Mountain rocks like spiritual champions and muses,
Mountain face like a god's castle,
Mountain slope like a mother's lap,
Mountain right like a banner unfurled,
Mountain left like a lotus in bloom.

Leaves on trees like goddesses making offerings.
Tree buds like ambrosial fruits.
Ponds and streams like a sacrificial vase.

Tiger and other beasts are like guard dogs.
Birds and deer are like farm animals.
Monkeys large and small are like neighbors.

Rainbows and fog are like a river headwater.
Gentle rain is like a shower of offerings.
Meadow and flowers are like a mandala.

In such a place of solitude,
The gods touch me, the mentor provides,
The muses enchant me, meditation deities encircle me.
Spiritual practice occurs naturally, through no effort on
    my part.
Sinful behavior ceases innately, through no effort on
    my part.

In future days whoever strives for enlightenment
Should rely on a place like this and meditate
    unwaveringly.
My children staying here, my students,
Look at the truth of your contemplative joy, and this will
    be clear.

Meditation Experience Flashes

When I am in the presence of my mentor,
Meditation experience flashes like a sharp weapon.
Yogin who no longer overstresses outer and inner
    events—what a joy.
This uncontrived thinking is itself Buddha.

When I am among my friends.
Meditation experience flashes like a mirror of clear
    appearances.
Yogin who clearly recalls advice—what a joy.

When I am on the snowy mountain peak,
Meditation experience flashes like a white lion.
Yogin who transcends what appears to be wholly other—
    what a joy.

When I am at the top of White Rock
Meditation experience flashes like a vulture.
Yogin who cuts through anything with ease—what a joy.

When I am in the mire of cyclic life,
Meditation experience flashes like a lotus flower.
Yogin who is unsullied by the faults of cyclic life—what
   a joy.

When I am amidst worldly ways,
Meditation experience flashes like a silver conch shell.
Yogin who is not bound up in material life—what a joy.

When I wander without aim through the land,
Meditation experience flashes like a tiger-stripe bee.
Yogin who does not long for objects of desire—what a joy.

This uncontrived thinking is Buddhahood itself.

Sources

All works on meditation presented in this anthology are translations from Tibetan-language texts composed by Tibetan Buddhist writers. This list provides details of the editions from which these translations were made. Other editions are available at the Buddhist Digital Resource Center (bdrc .io) or research libraries around the world. Previous translations, where they exist, are listed in Suggestions for Further Reading. Finally, a small selection of Tibetan-language Buddhist texts on meditation and related topics are included for those who want to pursue further readings.

INTRODUCTION

Dudjom Rinpoche: Bdud 'joms 'Jigs bral ye shes rdo rje (1904–1987). *Zab gsang mkha' 'gro'i snying thig gi sngon 'gro'i khrid rim thar lam snang sgron.* In *The Collected Writings and Revelations of H. H. Bdud-'joms rin-po-che 'jigs-bral-ye-shes-rdo-rje.* Kalimpog, India: Dupjung Lama: 1979–1985. Vol. 13, pp. 25–418, 401.2–402.3.

CHAPTER ONE:
TO THE MOUNTAIN

Zhabs dkar Tshogs drug rang grol (1781–1851). *Bya btang tshogs drug rang grol gyis rang dang skal ldan gdul bya la mgrin pa gdams pa'i bang mdzod nas glu dbyangs dga' ston 'gyes pa rnams*. In *Rje zhabs dkar tshogs drug rang grol gyi gsung 'bum*. Xining: Mtsho sngon mi rigs dpe skrun khang, 2002. Vol. 3, pp. 138.4–139.14, and 230.8–230.19.

Zhabs dkar Tshogs drug rang grol (1781–1851). *Bya btang tshogs drug rang grol gyis rang dang skal ldan gdul bya la mgrin pa gdams pa'i bang mdzod nas glu dbyangs dga' ston 'gyes pa rnams*. In *Rje zhabs dkar tshogs drug rang grol gyi gsung 'bum*. Xining: Mtsho sngon mi rigs dpe skrun khang, 2002. Vol. 4, pp. 685.1–686.12.

CHAPTER TWO:
AT THE FOOT OF THE TREE

Ta'a la'i bla ma 13 Thub bstan rgya mtsho (1876–1933). *Mdo smad sku 'bum byams gling dang / lha ldan cho 'phrul smon lam chen mo bcas kyi tshogs mgron du phebs skabs skyes rabs sogs kyi gsung bshad ljags bsgrigs*. In *Rgyal ba thub bstan rgya mtsho'i gsung 'bum*. New Delhi: International Academy of Indian Culture, 1981–1982. Vol. 2, pp. 163.5–173.1.

CHAPTER THREE:
LIVING AND DYING

Ye shes rgyal mtshan (1713–1793). *Byang chub lam gyi rim pa'i snying po bsdus pa dngos grub kun 'byung*. In *The Collected Works of the Tshe-mchog-glin yons-'dzin ye-ses-rgyal-mtshan*. New Delhi: Tibet House Library, 1974. Vol. 8, pp. 457–494. Selection: pp. 473.3–484.1.

CHAPTER FOUR:
SONGS OF IMPERMANENCE

Zhabs dkar Tshogs drug rang grol (1781–1851). *Bya btang tshogs drug rang grol gyis rang dang skal ldan gdul bya la mgrin pa gdams pa'i bang mdzod nas glu dbyangs dga' ston 'gyes pa rnams*.

Edited by Rdo rje tshe ring. Xining: Mtsho sngon mi rigs dpe skrun khang, 1987–1988. Vol. 1, pp. 153.16, 191.3, and 496.

Zhabs dkar Tshogs drug rang grol (1781–1851). *Bya btang tshogs drug rang grol gyis rang dang skal ldan gdul bya la mgrin pa gdams pa'i bang mdzod nas glu dbyangs dga' ston 'gyes pa rnams*. Edited by Rdo rje tshe ring. Xining: Mtsho sngon mi rigs dpe skrun khang, 1987–1988. Vol. 2, pp. 246, 257.8, and 346.2.

CHAPTER FIVE:
INNER CALM

Ngor chen Dkon mchog lhun grub (1497–1557). *Lam gyi sngon 'gro'i khrid yig snang gsum mdzes par byed pa'i rgyan*. In *E waṁ bka' 'bum*. Edited by Dpal brtsegs bod yig dpe rnying dpe skrun khang. Lhasa: Krung go'i bod rig pa dpe skrun khang, 2010. Vol. 13, pp. 154.9–166.8.

CHAPTER SIX:
WIDER PERSPECTIVE

Karma pa 9 Dbang phyug rdo rje (1556–1603). *Phyag rgya then po ma rig mun sel*. In *Phyag chen rgyas pa nges don rgya mtsho, 'bring po ma rig mun sel, bsdus pa chos sku mdzub tshugs*. Varanasi, U.P., India: Vajra Vidya Institute Library, n.d.; pp. 222.1–239.18.

CHAPTER SEVEN:
OURSELVES AND OTHERS

Gzhan phan chos kyi snang ba (1871–1927). *Byang chub sems dpa'i spyod pa la 'jug pa zhes bya ba'i mchan 'grel*. In Rgya kong mkhan chen gzhan phan chos kyi snang ba, editor, *Gsung 'bum gzhan phan chos kyi snang ba*. Rdzong sar: Rdzong sar khams bye'i slob gling, 2004. Vol. 2, pp. 149.5–159.5.

CHAPTER EIGHT:
COSMIC LOVE

Ngag dbang yon tan rgya mtsho (1928–2002). *Las dang po pa rnams las dam chos blo la 'dzin bde nyung bsdus.* In *Rje ngag dbang yon tan bzang po'i gsung 'bum phyogs bsgrigs.* 'Dzam thang: Mdo smad 'dzam thang 'jam dbyangs shes rig lte gnas. Vol. 8, pp. 1–266. Selection: pp. 226.9–233.18 and 235.1–238.4.

CHAPTER NINE:
OPEN MIND, VAST MIND

Dpal sprul O rgyan 'jigs med chos kyi dbang po. *Mthar thug rdzogs pa chen po sangs rgyas pa'i thabs zab mo bsgom pa rang grol.* In *Dpal sprul o rgyan 'jigs med chos kyi dbang po'i gsung 'bum.* Chengdu: Si khron mi rigs dpe skrun khang, 2009. Vol. 8, pp. 319–338.

CHAPTER TEN:
PLACES OF SOLITUDE

Klong chen rab 'byams (1308–1364). *Kun mkhyen klong chen rab 'byams kyi gsung 'bum.* Edited by Dpal brtsegs bod yig dpe rnying zhib 'jug khang. Beijing: Krung go'i bod rig pa dpe skrun khang, 2009. Vol. 22, pp. 201–208.

CHAPTER ELEVEN:
THE TRIALS OF SOLITUDE

Zhabs dkar Tshogs drug rang grol (1781–1851). *Bya btang tshogs drug rang grol gyis rang dang skal ldan gdul bya la mgrin pa gdams pa'i bang mdzod nas glu dbyangs dga' ston 'gyes pa rnams.* Edited by Rdo rje tshe ring. Xining: Mtsho sngon mi rigs dpe skrun khang, 1987–1988. Vol. 1, pp. 539.8–557.17.

CHAPTER TWELVE:
SHEER JOY

Karma pa 3 Rang byung rdo rje (1284–1339). *Rnal 'byor gyi dbang phyug mi la bzhad pa'i rdo rje'i gsung mgur mdzod nag ma.* Chengdu: Si khron mi rigs dpe skrun khang, 2008. Vol. 1, pp. 163.5, 187.5, 240.13, 257.12, and 286.1.

Karma pa 3 Rang byung rdo rje (1284–1339). *Rnal 'byor gyi dbang phyug mi la bzhad pa'i rdo rje'i gsung mgur mdzod nag ma.* Chengdu: Si khron mi rigs dpe skrun khang, 2008. Vol. 2, pp. 503.4 and 728.9.

Suggestions for Further Reading

Dakpo Tashi Namgyal. *Moonbeams of Mahāmudrā*. Translated by Elizabeth M. Callahan. Boulder, CO: Snow Lion, 2019. This encyclopedic work by Dakpo Tashi Namgyal (1512–1587) is the most extensive presentation of calm and insight meditation from the perspective of the Kagyu School.

Deshung Rinpoche. *The Three Levels of Spiritual Perception: A Commentary on the Three Visions*. Translated by Jared Rhoton. Somerville, MA: Wisdom Publications, 2003. This is a translation of the commentary on Ngorchen's *Beautiful Ornament of the Three Visions* by the twentieth-century writer Deshung Rinpoche's (1906–1987), containing useful explanations of the section on calm meditation (pp. 351–387).

Dudjom Rinpoche. *The Torch Lighting the Way to Freedom: Complete Instructions on the Preliminary Practices*. Translated by Padmakara Translation Group. Boston: Shambhala Publications, 2011. A classic twentieth-century text on the Buddhist foundation practices.

Longchenpa. *Finding Rest in Meditation: Trilogy of Rest* (previous translation). Translated by Padmakara Translation Group. Boulder, CO: Shambhala Publications, 2018. Vol. 2, pp. 40–55. This is a translation of Longchen Rabjam's verse text on meditation as well as his own commentary on that text. This is part of a three-volume work on mind, meditation, and the nature of illusion.

Longchenpa. *Kindly Bent to Ease Us*. Translated by Herbert V. Guenther. Berkeley: Dharma Publishing, 1975. 3 vols. This is a translation of the verse-text of Longchen Rabjam's trilogy, with extensive notes and fascinating commentary by the translator, Herbert Guenther. This and the later translation from the Padmakara Translation Group could be read together to highlight how much translation makes a difference for interpretation.

Milarepa. *The Hundred Thousand Songs of Milarepa: A New Translation.* Translated by Christopher Stagg. Boulder, CO: Shambhala Publications, 2017. This is Milarepa's major collection of songs and stories. This is perhaps best read along with *The Life of Milarepa.*

Milarepa. *The Life of Milarepa.* Translated by Andrew Quintman. New York: Penguin Classics, 2010. The most important narrative by Tibet's most famous poet-saint, Milarepa. This is essential reading for anyone interested in the Buddhist contemplative culture of Tibet.

Ngorchen Könchok Lhündrup. *The Beautiful Ornament of the Three Visions: Fundamental Teachings of the Sakya Lineage of Tibetan Buddhism* (previous translation). Translated by Lobsang Dagpa and Jay Goldberg. Ithaca, NY: Snow Lion Publications, 1991; pp. 157–171.

The Ninth Kar-ma-pa Wang-ch'ug Dor-je. *The Mahāmudrā Eliminating the Darkness of Ignorance, with Commentary Given Orally by Beru Khyentze Rinpoche* (previous translation). Translated by Alexander Berzin. Dharamsala, India: Library of Tibetan Works and Archives, 1978; pp. 43–65. See more recent volume on previous page, Dakpo Tashi Namgyal, *Moonbeams of Mahāmudrā*, pp. 489–533.

Patrul Rinpoche. *The Words of My Perfect Teacher.* Boston: Shambhala Publications, 1998. The most popular and lively foundation practice text in English translation, representing the viewpoint of the Nyingma School. This provides useful background and depth for any of the topics treated here.

Shabkar. *The Life of Shabkar: The Autobiography of a Tibetan Yogin.* Translated by Matthieu Ricard, Jakob Leschly, Erik Schmidt, Marilyn Silverstone, and Lodrö Palmo. Stony Brook, NY: State University of New York Press, 1994. The autobiography of Shabkar Tsokdruk Rangdröl (1781–1851), covering the first half of his life and including many spiritual songs and stories of his contemplative retreats throughout the Himalayas.

Shabkar. *Songs of Shabkar: The Path of a Tibetan Yogi Inspired by Nature.* Translated by Victoria Sujata. Cazadero, CA: Dharma Publications, 2012. Translations of a selection of Shabkar's poems.

Lama Shabkar. "Self-Liberated Mind." In *The Flight of the Garuda* (previous translation). Translated by Erik Pema Kunsang. Kathmandu: Rangjung Yeshe Publications, 1986; pp. 147–163.

Shabkar Tsogdruk Rangdrol. *The Emanated Scripture of Manjushri: Shabkar's Essential Meditation Instructions.* Translated by Sean Price. Boulder, CO: Snow Lion Publications, 2020. This text by Shabkar is a very readable survey of the Buddhist path, based upon the structure of Tsongkhapa's more complex *Stages of the Path*. It includes chapters on most of the topics discussed in this anthology.

Shantideva. *The Way of the Bodhisattva*. Translated by Padmakara Translation Group. Boulder, CO: Shambhala Publications, 1997. A beautiful translation of the seventh-century Indian Buddhist classic. Chapter 8 is on meditation, while chapters 1 through 7 resonate with the foundation practices featured in this anthology.

Taranatha. *Essence of Ambrosia: A Guide to Buddhist Contemplations*. Translated by Willa Baker. Dharmsala, India: Library of Tibetan Works and Archives, 2005. A foundation practice text from Ngawang Yönten Gyatso's tradition, the Jonang School, and a source for portions of the work presented here.

Tenzin Chögyel. *The Life of the Buddha*. Translated by Kurtis R. Schaeffer. New York: Penguin Classics, 2015. A life of the Buddha written in Bhutan during the eighteenth century. This includes the story of the Buddha's meditation seat that the Thirteenth Dalai Lama tells.

The Thirteenth Dalai Lama. *The Path of the Bodhisattva Warrior*. Translated by Glenn H. Mullin (previous translation). Ithaca, NY: Snow Lion Publications, 1988; pp. 171–182.

Thupten Jinpa. *Songs of Spiritual Experience: Tibetan Buddhist Poems of Insight and Awakening*. Translated with Jaś Elsner. Boulder, CO: Shambhala Publications, 2014. This is a very readable anthology of Tibetan Buddhist poetry, including a generous selection of poems on impermanence.

Tshe-mchog-gling. *Ye-shes-rgyal-mtshan*. *Mind in Buddhist Psychology*. Translated by Herbert V. Guenther and Leslie S. Kawamura. Emeryville, CA: Dharma Publishing, 1975. This book contains a translation of Yeshé Gyeltsen's brief text on the classification of feelings, emotions, and types of thought, "The Necklace of Clear Understanding." While not about meditation per se, this text presents the kind of descriptive analysis of mind and thought that goes hand in hand with insight meditation, providing a detailed survey of what one might expect to find when interrogating one's own mind during insight practice.

Tsongkhapa. *The Great Treatise on the Stages of the Path to Enlightenment*. Translated by the Lamrim Chenmo Translation Committee. 3 vols. Ithaca, NY: Snow Lion Publications, 2000. This magnum opus of Tsongkhapa Losang Drakpa (1357–1419) is the most important presentation of Buddhist thought and practice in the Geluk School, the school of the Dalai Lama. It contains extensive and philosophically dense chapters on calm and insight meditation.

Wallace, B. Alan. *Balancing the Mind: A Tibetan Buddhist Approach to Refining Attention.* Ithaca, NY: Snow Lion Publications, 2005. This contains a translation of a chapter on calm meditation in Tsongkhapa's *Smaller Treatise on the Stages of the Path to Enlightenment* (pp. 104–221). This is interspersed with Wallace's commentary, though Tsongkhapa's text may be read separately. This work is more approachable than Tsongkhapa's *Great Treatise*. Together, they illustrate the sophisticated philosophical discussion that went hand in hand with calm meditation in the Geluk School.

The Life of the Buddha

Translated with an Introduction by Kurtis R. Schaeffer

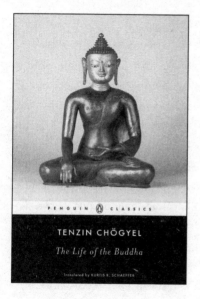

The story of Shakyamuni Buddha's epic journey to enlightenment is perhaps the most important narrative in the Buddhist tradition. Tenzin Chögyel's *The Life of the Buddha*, composed in the mid-eighteenth century and now in a vivid translation, is a storyteller's rendition of the twelve acts of the Buddha. This classical tale has the power to engage people through a deeply human story with cosmic implications.

The Life of Milarepa

Translated by Andrew Quintman
Introduction by Donald S. Lopez, Jr.

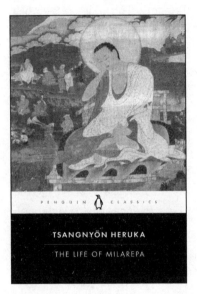

The Life of Milarepa, a biography and a dramatic tale from a culture now in crisis, can be read on several levels. A personal and moving introduction to Tibetan Buddhism, it is also a detailed guide to the search for liberation. It presents a quest for purification and buddhahood in a single lifetime, tracing the path of a great sinner who became a great saint while also reflecting the religious and social life of medieval Tibet.

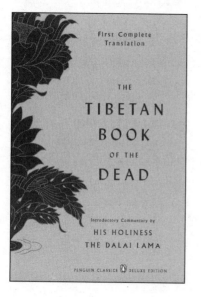

The All-Pervading Melodious Drumbeat

The Life of Ra Lotsawa

Translated with an Introduction by Bryan J. Cuevas

RA YESHÉ SENGÉ

The All-Pervading Melodious Drumbeat

The Life of Ra Lotsawa

Though he was canonized as an enlightened buddha, Ra Lotsawa Dorjé Drak used his magical abilities to defeat rivals, accumulate wealth, and amass a following. His life offers a view into the overlooked roles of magic and sorcery in the Buddhist tradition. Despite this sinister legacy, his fame also rests on an illustrious career as a translator of Buddhist scriptures, through which he helped spark a renaissance of Buddhism in Tibet.